Derek Tangye and his wife left their glamorous existence in London when they discovered Minack, a deserted cottage close to the cliffs of Mount's Bay. Jeannie gave up her job as Press Relations Officer of the Savoy Hotel Group and Derek resigned from MI5. They then proceeded to carve from the wild land around the cottage the meadows which became their flower farm.

Derek has become famous all over the world for his series of bestsellers about this flower farm in Cornwall, The Minack Chronicles. Jeannie, who illustrated these books with charming line drawings, died in 1986 – and this is her story.

Also by Derek Tangye:

The Minack Chronicles:

Derek Tangye

JEANNIE
A Love Story

WARNER BOOKS

A *Warner* Book

First published in Great Britain by Michael Joseph Ltd, 1988
Published by Sphere Books Ltd 1989
Reprinted 1989, 1990, 1991
Reprinted by Warner Books 1993
Reprinted 1994, 1995

ISBN 0 7515 0756 3

Printed in England by Clays Ltd, St Ives plc

Warner Books
A Division of
Little, Brown and Company (UK)
Brettenham House
Lancaster Place
London WC2E 7EN

To Barbara
and all those who knew Jeannie

ONE

Twelfth Night. The frolic is over, reality has taken its place. Twelfth Night has always seemed to me to be a sad time, bringing apprehension.

'Aren't we lucky,' said Jeannie, 'to have each other?'

'Aren't we lucky?' was a phrase used often by Jeannie. It was a mirror of her personality. She never took happiness for granted.

'Fred had a wonderful life,' she added, gently.

We had finished taking down the Christmas cards, and Jeannie was on her hands and knees, picking up the drawing pins which had fallen to the carpet after I had plucked the cards from the ceiling beams.

'I wouldn't like Ambrose or Cherry to step on them,' she had said. And I had laughed . . . 'You don't think of my bare feet!'

I, a one-time cat-hater, have been pursued by cats since I married Jeannie.

First there was Monty of *A Cat in the Window* whom I first met in Room 205 of the Savoy Hotel, Jeannie's office when she was Publicity Officer for the Savoy Hotel, Claridge's and the Berkeley. He was then a kitten, the colour of autumn bracken. After our London years he came with us to Minack; and now he lies buried beside the little stream which crosses the lane at the entrance to Minack, known as Monty's Leap.

I

Then there was Lama who arrived a few months after Monty had died, after I had sworn that I would never agree to have another cat. I did, however, add a proviso. I said that I would accept one 'if it came to the door in a storm, and was black'. Lama came to the door in a storm, *and* was black.

Next there was Oliver, who was also black. Strange, but even in my anti-cat days I had respect for a black cat. I always felt pleased if a black cat crossed my path. We first saw Oliver in a corner of the field on the other side of the valley; and during the following months he haunted the cottage surroundings as if he believed he belonged here. Lama was alive then, and we did not like another cat disturbing her, so I used to make horrid noises to frighten him away. But Oliver produced an ace card.

I was standing one Sunday by Monty's Leap when, to my amazement, there appeared out of the undergrowth on the other side of the gate, a tiny, autumn-bracken-colour kitten, the exact replica of Monty as a kitten; and it was followed out of the undergrowth by Oliver.

'If you feed that kitten,' I said to Jeannie in mock rage, 'I'll leave you!'

Of course she did; and so Oliver and Ambrose came into our lives.

We now call the other side of the valley Oliver land, because of that time we first saw him. It is there, too, that lies the Ambrose Rock, so named because, after we had bought the twenty acres of land which goes down to the sea and includes Carn Barges from where we first saw Minack, Ambrose came for a walk with us, jumped on this rock, and purred. We had a drama buying this land. We bought it just in time. It was going to be 'developed'. And I tell that story in *The Ambrose Rock*.

Ambrose was on his own for a long while after Oliver died. Then one day, one misty day, Jeannie found a little cat, skin and bone, not more than six months old, curled at the bottom of the cherry tree. And it was black, black as black can be when seen from a short distance, but having, here and there, touches of apricot fur. Like the others, we have never found where Cherry came from.

It was now four in the afternoon and growing dark, and I switched on the lamp which was standing on the little table beside the sofa – the sofa which had been part of all our married life, part of my bachelor life before I met Jeannie.

'I think I'll go and see Merlin,' I said.

'Where is he?'

'He was in the stable meadow when I last saw him.'

'Poor Merlin.'

I did not go straight to the stable meadow. Instead I walked the few paces from the cottage door up the incline to the bridge, the patio which resembles the bridge of a ship as you stand there looking out upon the sea of Mount's Bay, the line of the Lizard stretching out like a pointing figure in the distance. I have spent much time there, still do, thinking over problems; or sometimes I stand there with my mind blank, wasting time a practical person might say, and yet wisdom may emerge from such silent moments. Thoughts come welling up from within you, spontaneously, often surprising you.

I stood there on the bridge, and was aware of simple things. A male chaffinch with faded plumage hopped from branch to branch of the hornbeams on my right, hoping I had crumbs to give him, and I called out:

'Patience, Charlie, I'll get something for you in a minute.'

Ever since the first male chaffinch made an impact

3

on our imaginations by the way he followed us about, all the male chaffinches have been called Charlie.

Above me, like a moving parade of gliders, gulls silently floated across the dying light of the sky, west to east because they knew a gale was blowing up from the west, and they would have shelter under the cliffs of the east.

An oystercatcher flew nearby which I could not see, but I heard its weird, lonely piping cry, as if it represented a drowning sailor calling for help.

I stood there pondering about the events of the past few days.

I heard an owl hoot to the left of me in the wood, close by, probably in a tree by the small greenhouse; and it was answered a few seconds later by another at the other end of the wood.

I saw the port light of a fishing boat heading for Newlyn, close in-shore because I lost sight of the light as she passed the rocks of Carn Barges, the rocks which resemble an ancient sea castle falling to the sea's edge; Carn Barges from where Jeannie and I first saw Minack.

A breeze, stirring suddenly, advance guard of what the gliding gulls had foretold, touched the leaves of the escallonia beside me and reminded me of July summer days when honeybees filled the pink flowers of the escallonia with their hum.

The caressing murmur of the sea had begun to change its tone. Around me it was becoming dark, not because the day was running out of its time, but because of the grey clouds, balloons of scudding clouds, each with a design that no professional designer could have achieved. A vast canopy of nature encompassed me as I stood on the bridge.

And, in this arena where all was natural, I began to reflect about what had happened four days before; and which, I subconsciously knew, was going to be the changing point in our lives.

On Christmas Eve it was our custom to give homemade mincepies to the donkeys. The custom began when at one lunchtime pub session we met an old man who told us, with such sincerity that we believed him, that donkeys knelt down on their knees when twelve o'clock came on Christmas Eve. At this time we had recently acquired two donkeys.

We had visited a pub one evening called the Plume of Feathers, at Scorrier, near Redruth. The landlord was a round Dickensian figure who was a cattle dealer,

a horse and donkey dealer as well as being a 'mine host'. Indeed he was ready to sell anything which he thought was saleable; and when I admired a mat in the saloon bar, he quickly said:

'I'll sell it to you. What will you offer?'

Jeannie had always wanted a donkey: a childhood dream since the days her family had holidays in the Isles of Scilly, and Jeannie used to pocket lumps of sugar from the breakfast table, then feed them to the donkeys who were plentiful at the time in the Scillies.

5

On the occasion of this visit she mentioned her dream to the Dickensian landlord, then thought little more about it. I, in fact, did not even know she had mentioned the subject to the landlord until, a week later, a telegram was delivered which read: 'Got donkey.'

Consternation on my part.

'What have you been up to?' I asked sternly.

'Nothing, nothing, I promise you. I just mentioned I loved donkeys.'

Understandably she was intrigued by the telegram, and I also was intrigued, enough to say, reluctantly, that we could at any rate go and find out what the donkey looked like.

So back we went in the evening to the Plume of Feathers; and we were greeted by the Dickensian landlord with such warmth that I found myself feeling I had been placed at a disadvantage. I was not in control. Jeannie was going to be charmed by his enthusiasm.

'She's a lovely little donkey,' he said, turning his charm on Jeannie. 'Needs a home badly. She was saved from the knacker's yard, may have to go back there. Can't keep her much longer . . .'

We had a couple of drinks, and I began to be more friendly.

Then Jeannie went off to see the donkey, tethered in a back yard; and she came back excited as a child.

I was still hesitant.

'Ah,' said the Dickensian landlord, thinking that he could influence me in the same way that he would have been influenced, 'you've got a bargain . . . the donkey is in foal! In a month you'll have two donkeys for the price of one!'

Then turning to the optic and offering me another drink, he added, with a twinkle in his eye: 'If you don't want the foal, I'll buy it back for £10 – a circus always likes to have a donkey foal!'

He didn't influence me.

My decision had been made.

All I wanted to do was to respond to the shine in Jeannie's eyes.

Thus Penny, then Fred came into our lives.

As I stood there on the bridge in the dying light, I saw the evening gull flying gently up the valley from the rocks, Lamorna way. It had no other name but the evening gull. It was always alone, always arriving at dusk, perching on the roof, noiseless, waiting for our attention.

I waited a few moments, then walked back to the cottage door, and called out to Jeannie: 'The evening gull is here. Can you give him something?'

And she called back to me: 'Yes . . . in a minute.'

Jeannie wanted to be a vet when she was a child. Lots of children, in fantasising their future, say they want to be vets; and I am sure Jeannie would have made an excellent vet, except for one weakness in her character. She would have become too involved with her patients. She would love them too much, worry about them too much, and, in a case of cruelty, she would lose her temper too much. I always had to cut out from the newspapers any unpleasant stories about an animal. She was not scared by such stories, just revolted; and she wondered despairingly how there could be a public to enjoy them.

Vets, unlike Jeannie, have to view such problems with detachment, have to remain uninvolved with the immense sadness an animal can cause. Yet vets seldom seem to follow such a role. They do often involve themselves; and the vets who have come to Minack have always done so. Especially in the case of Fred.

Fred's companion after Penny had died was Mingoose Merlin. Mingoose Merlin (so called after the village of Mingoose where he was born) was bought by us from a couple who lived at Skinners Bottom, a mile or two away from the Plume of Feathers pub near Scorrier, where Penny came from.

He was eighteen months old, and though he was funny to look at, he was an aristocratic donkey. Fred was a hill-billy donkey conceived by an unknown father among the hills of Connemara. Mingoose Merlin, on the other hand, had distinguished parents, both of whom had won many show prizes; their names, and also that of Merlin, are in the Donkey Breed Society Stud Book.

Merlin was funny to look at because of his shaggy chocolate brown coat, his stocky legs, which made him appear to be wearing old-fashioned plus-fours, and there was a fringe over his eyes like that which covers the eyes of an Old English Sheepdog. Merlin, when he was delivered, was taken out of the horsebox in which he had travelled, at the farm a quarter of a mile away from Minack; Jeannie took the lead of his halter, and they ran down the lane together, Merlin pulling all the way, as if he was coming home; and he jumped Monty's Leap, Jeannie hanging on, then past the stables to where Fred was waiting at the gate. From the moment of meeting they were friends.

The first time Merlin was introduced to the Christmas Eve ceremony, he spat the mincepie out of his mouth. The next Christmas he changed his mind about them; and on the Christmas Eve we had just passed, he had enjoyed Jeannie's homemade mincepies, just as much as Fred had done.

During the previous few months, Jeannie had had an intuitive sense of concern about Fred. Fancifully she had been saying to me that he was missing Penny. I remember the night Penny had become ill. Fred had, in the middle of the night, jumped a hedge and raced to the porch door and bellowed.

8

Even in retrospect, however, neither of us could say that Fred was off colour on Christmas Eve, or any of the following days up to New Year's Eve. Indeed, friends had an hilarious time with him and Merlin on the 29th. Hilarious because they were in the donkey field above the cottage, and there was a thick mist, and they wanted a photograph of both donkeys together . . . but as soon as they got one donkey in camera view, the other one disappeared in the mist.

They had a photograph also of Fred pushing his nose into the Christmas tree which stood lighted in the porch. All his life it had been a party trick for Fred to come into the porch. If we had a lunch party, a tea party, I would at some stage disappear to fetch Fred from wherever he might be, and lead him back to the cottage; and then, when I came close to the cottage, I would take off his halter and let him run. He knew what he had to do. He would race round the corner by the water butt, and arrive with a flourish at the porch door, where he would be greeted with delighted cries from our guests: 'Look at Fred!' And Fred, the door open, would push his nose towards the table where a cake was quickly cut and a piece given to him.

On the 30th in the late afternoon, neither Fred or Merlin showed any wish to leave the donkey field where they had spent the day, no wish to come with me down to the stables; and as it was a warm, still evening, we let them be.

I woke next morning, however, with an uneasy feeling about Fred, and when I told Jeannie this, she said, in a practical fashion, that the only way to rid myself of such a feeling was to get up and prove that the unease was due to my imagination. So I got up, leaving Jeannie in bed with Ambrose curled beside her.

There was no sign of Fred or Merlin in the donkey

field. The field has, however, a gap at the far end which leads into a meadow surrounded by trees, a meadow which was a bog when first we came to Minack; and which, after much effort, we at last succeeded in draining by digging ditches and lining them with earthenware pipes, and covering them up. It so happened that Alan Whicker, the television commentator, came to Minack to interview us when *A Gull on the Roof* was published, and at the time I was in the process of digging the ditches. So somewhere in the BBC archives there is a film of me at work in this meadow, where I was about to find Fred and Merlin.

The meadow is now the home of Joseph MacLeod daffodils in one half, and an assorted number of other daffodils in the other half. Each autumn, I cut down the undergrowth, and by Christmas I have usually wired off the gap so that the donkeys do not damage the daffodil spikes as they begin to grow. This year, for some idle reason, I had delayed doing so; and so when I reached the gap, I knew the donkeys would be somewhere around.

I did not see Merlin, but I saw Fred; and immediately alarm bells rang.

He was in the centre of the meadow, standing quite still.

'Fred!' I called out, as I walked towards him. 'What's wrong old boy?'

He shuffled his feet.

'Come on, Fred, what's wrong?'

Yesterday he looked normal. Today he seemed to me to look thin.

I tried to move him, tried to persuade him to come back with me, and then I would have led him down to the shelter of the stables. But he wouldn't move; and so I went back alone to tell Jeannie.

'You go and phone Paul,' she said, 'and I'll go and stay with Fred.'

TWO

Paul was our vet, and because we had no telephone I had to drive to a call-box five minutes away at a hamlet incongruously called Sheffield.

There was a weak moment in our lives when we thought of having a telephone installed, and we made enquiries which resulted in two telephone engineers coming to see us, and offering to connect us for £75. They had visited us before the post arrived.

When the post came, however, there was a letter from Jeannie's very charming sister, a telephone queen, who said she was thrilled at the prospect of us being on the telephone because she then could have plenty of nice chats. The prospect alarmed us, reminding us also that we were once telephone addicts; and we realised that, the world dialling system being so easy, we would soon be finding ourselves dialling our friends around the world. Our telephone account would be enormous.

'And,' Jeannie added, 'we are both inclined to be volatile. We would start saying things on the telephone which we would never say in a letter after we had time to think.'

Jeannie was delightfully volatile. It was part of her charm, part of the wild Celtic dash in her character which made some people say they thought of a Brontë character when they thought of Jeannie, a girl of the

Cornish moors in place of the Yorkshire moors; and there were others, as I did myself, who saw in Jeannie the passion of Scarlett O'Hara of *Gone with the Wind*.

I had to restrain her sometimes. She had a single-mindedness about her love for Minack; and I had a name for her, F.E. Jeannie. I used also to call my mother, when she was alive, an F.E. mother; and sometimes Jeannie and my mother would combine their F.E. attitudes. For F.E. stood for Fire Eating, two words I chose after they were on the verge of embarking upon a quite unnecessary F.E. episode.

It was close to the beginning of our life at Minack. There was no lane to reach our cottage from the farm at the top of the hill. The only way to reach us was across two fields. Hence we proceeded to create a lane, and at some expense.

One day when my mother was staying with us, and the new lane had just been opened up, we looked out of the window and saw that the first person using it was a neighbour. Frankly, he had every right to use it because, at that time, he had cliff land beyond Minack. True it was irritating that he was using our lane instead of going, as previously, across the fields, but I myself could not blame him for doing this.

Not so the F.E. couple, my mother and Jeannie. They were enraged that after all our work, after all the expense, they had to look out of the window and see our neighbour exploiting our efforts.

They wanted to rush out and stop him.

'Take a deep breath,' I said to them both. 'Keep calm.'

I have, however, my own F.E. moments. They simmer to a boiling point, slowly. I feel that I am being made use of, or being deceived by smiles or, when there is a crunch, that people whom I treated as friends turn out to be only fair-weather friends . . . and it is then that I momentarily erupt, like when a pressure cooker releases its steam. The victim is astonished.

My mother adored Jeannie. So did my father, who only knew her for a brief while. My mother said that Jeannie looked like a pocket Venus. My father happened to be in London the night when Jeannie and I got engaged.

I had been told that I would soon have to leave the house where Jeannie and I lived, Cholmondley House just below Richmond Bridge; so we set out to find another house also on the river, and we found one on Chiswick Mall called Gothic Cottage. It was ideal but I felt it would be unfair on Jeannie to live there unless I was married to her. In those days nosy neighbours were influenced by Church idealism. So while we inspected Gothic Cottage, I privately decided that I was going to propose to Jeannie. I would wait, I decided, till the evening.

I had made a date to meet her in the Coalhole, the pub next door to the Savoy Theatre, because I knew she was having drinks in the Savoy bar with Leslie Mitchell, the BBC star news announcer of the time, and I did not want to interfere.

I sat there in the Coalhole at a table with a marble top, waiting, waiting, and ruminating about my future relationship with Jeannie; perhaps I should change my mind, and not propose.

She was an hour late. She came up to me, smiling deliciously, handing me a bottle of Savoy whisky (whisky was gold at the time).

'Penance money,' she said provocatively, handing me the bottle.

I proposed to her after that and, startled, she accepted.

'Anyone could have knocked me over with a tap,' she said later.

13

We were due to have dinner with my father that evening and I knew he would not fail me with his enthusiasm. We had dinner at a restaurant then called the Good Intent in the King's Road, near to my one-time mews flat in Elm Park Lane. We had a wonderfully happy time; and at the end of the evening when I was alone with my father, he said:

'You have a winner.'

Fred still had not moved by the time the vet arrived. He stood there, occasionally shuffling his feet, and I posed the possibility to the vet that laminitis was the cause of the trouble. Laminitis is a fever of the feet, brought on by eating too much lush grass.

'Not at this time of the year,' the vet replied, 'there's no bite in the grass.'

He proceeded to examine Fred's feet nevertheless, probing with a special instrument to see if a pebble had got lodged in one of the feet. He found nothing. Indeed, having examined him extensively, he said he could find nothing wrong with him. He then suggested we contact a farrier. It was his opinion that the paring of Fred's feet might help him.

'I'll be off for a couple of days,' he added, 'but my colleague will come out at any time you need him.'

We were sorry about this – not that we had any need to be sorry as it turned out. But it was New Year's Eve, and both were remembering Penny, and how Penny, nine years before, also became ill on New Year's Eve ... and how then, just as now, we had felt inhibited by the ambiance of New Year's Eve. Call out a vet or a doctor on New Year's Eve? It seemed unfair, and it might be unnecessary, a false alarm, and then the doctor or vet concerned would have had the rhythm of his New Year's Eve broken. Silly to feel like that.

As soon as the vet had gone, we hastened to find our regular farrier, and this meant driving to Halsetown near St Ives where he lived. And we had the luck of finding him at home; and he said he would come immediately. We felt relieved. We felt good fortune was on our side, and that all would now be well.

Fred was still where we left him, but after the farrier had gone to work on his feet, a miracle seemed to occur. Fred began moving about quite normally, and when I put the halter on him, he made no protest about coming with me across the field towards the cottage, through the gate, down the path, and then into the paddock in front of the stable. Jeannie and I were elated. We could now celebrate New Year's Eve ourselves.

Then came a warning note.

'Something basic wrong,' said our farrier, who was tall and dark, and full of memories of his childhood with donkeys and horses in the bogs of his home in Northern Ireland.

'He needs feeding up quick,' he said, 'not just with carrots – better feed him up with pony pellets.'

So off I went again, this time to Penzance to buy a sack of pony pellets.

I came back, filled the palm of my hand with pellets, and pressed Fred to have them. Reluctantly he accepted a few. Jeannie offered him a cut-up carrot, and he reluctantly accepted that too.

'Good sign,' I said.

'Oh darling,' Jeannie replied, 'I hope so.'

I remembered, as she spoke, that day when she carried Fred, born in the field through which now goes the coastal path, to the stables, Penny following her. I remembered the moment when Fred escaped from the stables, still a wobbling foal, and put his head through *The Times* which Jeannie's mother was reading as she

15

sat on the white seat a few yards away. I remembered
that Fred was at first thought to be a girl, and was
given the name of Marigold. I remembered all the
Christmas Eves as if they were fused into one, Fred
and Penny munching their mincepies by candlelight.

We stayed with him until long after dark, then went
to have supper, and came back again. He was standing
against the stone wall of the yard in front of the stable
door.

'Glad it's a warm night,' I said.

'Fantastically warm,' Jeannie replied.

Merlin was standing close by. He was anxious, I
could see that. He would spasmodically go up to Fred,
and nuzzle him, but Fred didn't seem to like him doing
so. Fred would back away or butt him with his head,
in the way that people are inclined to behave when
they do not wish to admit they are ill. 'Don't fuss me!'
is the watchword then.

We went to bed, then up at dawn, the first awakening
peaceful, a split second later the peace shattered by
fear.

It was a very beautiful dawn, very still, soft as a
spring dawn; and we walked down to the stables and
found Fred just where we had left him, standing
alongside the stone wall of the yard. Beyond this stone
wall one can see the sea, and on the horizon there was
the rising sun, an astonishing burgeoning of apricot
colours mingling with wisps of cloud; and as we stood
there watching and marvelling, stroking Fred, talking
to him, we became aware of a silhouette on the wall a
few feet away. It was Cherry, the little black cat which
Jeannie had found curled under the cherry tree opposite the stables, three months before; Cherry who had
been infiltrating into our lives ever since, contesting
with Ambrose for our affections.

'Oh that's lucky,' I said, who, although born a cat-hater, had always believed a black cat was an omen of good luck.

Cherry sat there watching Fred, close to a granite gatepost which had stood there for score upon score of years.

'Yes, that's lucky,' said Jeannie, although in her case she always believed that red was her lucky colour, and that seven was her lucky number.

'Are we doing everything we should do?' I said. 'I mean, we mustn't be mesmerised by New Year's Day.'

'Why not ask Margaret's advice?'

Margaret, who has for a long time helped us during the daffodil season and who, with George, her husband, has a pottery at the end of our lane; pottery which is world renowned for its exclusive, highly individual style. Margaret is also an experienced horsewoman.

'Ask her to come down and have a look at Fred. She's always loved him.'

Margaret was unavailable in the morning, but she arrived soon after lunchtime. An east wind had sprung up, and it had become colder. Jeannie or myself had been with Fred all morning, and we would try to persuade him to eat by pushing slivers of carrots into his mouth. He appeared to accept them, but only later did we discover that he never swallowed them, just kept them in the corner of his mouth. 'Didn't want to disappoint us,' said Jeannie.

Margaret was practical.

'You can't possibly leave him outside,' she said. 'We'll have to get him into the stable.'

He wouldn't move.

Jeannie put the halter on him while Margaret and I got between him and the wall and shoved at his hindquarters. Bit by bit he shuffled his way the few yards to the stable. He was weak. It was obvious we had to have the vet again as soon as possible. So off went Jeannie with Margaret to telephone.

Meanwhile I set out to create a makeshift door, for there was no normal stable door. Both Penny and Fred hated being shut in, however cold it was, and they kicked the door we originally had to pieces.

For Penny, when she became ill, I had made the same kind of makeshift door I now proceeded to make for Fred. I hung a curtain of old blankets to cover the door space; and I pulled across the lower half of the door space an iron slide. An iron slide, before the age of bulldozers, was used to shift rocks from one part of a field to another: the rock was manoeuvred on to the slide which was then chained to a horse or a tractor and pulled away. The slide was heavy. It was difficult for a donkey to shift. Penny tried to do so in the last early morning of her life. I had woken up, hearing the sound of banging. The time was half past five. The day was 2 January, nine years before.

The vet arrived, colleague of our usual vet, and proceeded to take Fred's temperature, examine his eyes, look at his throat and make various tests; and he could not find a hint of what might be wrong. 'I'm baffled,' he said.

He went away, saying he would return at eleven o'clock that night; and Jeannie said to me how lucky that we had someone who cared so much for an animal he had never met before, offering to come back, not being asked.

There was a pile of bracken, brought in at the end of summer for bedding, heaped at one end of the stable; and after we had supper, Jeannie and I returned to the stable and lay down on this pile of bracken. We were to stay there until the vet returned, a calor-gas lamp creating a dim light, throwing shadows on the white-washed stone walls, hovering around other aspects of the stable like that of the loft. We lay there in the bracken, making fitful remarks, Fred in the corner facing us to the left, Merlin, a self-conscious Merlin who was at a loss to understand why we were there, in the opposite right hand corner.

'Monty loved the loft,' I said.

'His favourite hide-out.'

'You took such a risk that night you brought him here,' I mused.

It was before we had permanently settled at Minack. I had come down by car for a few days, and Jeannie was to join me by train at the weekend; and then we were going to drive back together.

Jeannie had various parties to go to that week, and at the final one she suddenly decided to bring Monty on her night journey to join me. It was during the period when an American magazine described her as 'the prettiest publicity girl in the world'.

A hired car took her back to Mortlake from the Savoy Hotel, then she searched for Monty, who was out in the garden. She found him, grabbed him, wrapped him in a rug, then proceeded in the car to Paddington Station, where she smuggled Monty into her sleeper.

I was on the platform of Penzance Station in the morning, and I saw her looking out of a carriage window beckoning me; and when I reached her, she led me to her compartment, and there was Monty on her bunk.

'The attendant didn't find him there till this morning!'

And she was laughing.

'Oh you are a darling, dangerous girl,' I said, hugging her.

We lay there in the bracken, staring up at the cobwebs among the rafters; and I thought of the swallows who had made their clay nests there during summer days. I saw a sheaf of raffia dangling from a corner of the loft, raffia which we once used for tying our freesia bunches. All sorts of reminders were in the loft which belonged to the period when Jeannie, weary of sophisticated life, had allied herself with me in trying to find a life which had true values.

We lay there in the bracken . . . and I heard Jeannie mumble to herself: 'Don't go Fred. Please don't go.'

The vet returned at eleven o'clock, and he decided to give Fred a 'drench', which consisted of glucose and nutritious vitamins put in a bottle then poured down the throat. This was performed without difficulty. Fred drank it all.

There was now nothing else to do except to wait and see what effect it might have; and the vet advised wrapping him in a blanket, then leaving him alone to have an undisturbed sleep.

This we did.

At half past five the following morning, we were woken by a sound, a clanging sound, of metal being banged. Just for a minute. Then silence.

It was the same sound that we heard when Penny had died. She had tried to escape, in her last moments, from the stable into the field. She belonged to the open world of nature, to the Connemara hills where she came from, not to the logical controlled world of a stable.

So too felt Fred.

We found him lying against the metal slide.

In the same place, at the same time, on the same date as Penny nine years before.

Jeannie had written the following lines about Penny. She had never read them to me. I later found them in her desk.

The spirits of Minack
Welcome you
To their world of Forever
Where life continues
And death is never.

THREE

I left the bridge, staying longer than I had intended. There was a sparkle of lights at intervals along the Lizard far away across the bay, and a pink glow above the land beside Porthleven where the Royal Naval Culdrose Air Station reigned; and the floodlights were shining on the satellite 'dishes' close by. The day was ending.

I went back to the cottage.

'How was Merlin?' asked Jeannie.

'Haven't seen him yet,' I said.

'Then what have you been doing?'

'Ruminating, just ruminating,' I replied.

She was wearing black, close-fitting slacks, and a red polo-neck jumper. She looked ageless. The slim figure of a young chorus girl, the untouched dark hair reaching her shoulders, the smooth skin . . . I thought how lucky I was to have a wife who was a partner in all our endeavours, a mistress, a companion so close that we had no need for outside company, and who was admired by so many.

'I have always been discreet,' said Jeannie mischievously once.

Neither of us in all the years we have been together has ever doubted that we would always be together. Boredom is the menace in a marriage, not infidelity. We have had our rows, of course, and sometimes I have wondered whether we would have stayed together had we remained in London. Too much stress. Too many temptations. Too many late nights, tired days. But here at Minack there has never been any doubt: any row we might have soon died away because of our isolation. No telephone with which one could fuel a row by talking to a sympathiser. We were a mile off the main road, and that blunted any prospect of fulfilling a threat like 'I'm leaving you!' Neither of us would relish carrying a suitcase that far.

'I've caught you in a web,' I would say sometimes jokingly to her. 'I'll never let you escape.'

She did, however, escape occasionally, going to London on her own, coming back brimful of stories as to what had happened to her. The stories were always full of fun. She cascaded fun, and she effortlessly conveyed this sense of fun in whatever circle she moved.

Yet I have never felt that I have really *known* her, and that is because of the contradictions in her character; and she has never really *known* me because of the contradictions in mine. That is what has made our companionship so exciting. We remained, in a way, strangers to each other. Every day was as if we had met for the first time. True we belonged totally to each other, but we maintained our independence. We were like two islands joined together by a bridge.

She was one of those rare persons who intuitively recognise the true values of life, and then have the courage to seek them. During her legendary time at the Savoy Hotel, described in her book *Meet Me at the Savoy*, she made friends with all those who came to her office at Room 205: journalists, film stars, politicians from every part of the world, because they knew they could trust her. They could confide, and the secret would be kept. She was a giver, not a taker.

She respected what she believed the Savoy Hotel represented. It represented, in her mind, standards of style, behaviour, and a dedication on the part of the staff to give a perfect service to the guests. She was not thinking in a commercial fashion. She believed that the maintenance of long-established standards was a basic ingredient for a non-violent civilisation. Only when standards are ridiculed does a civilisation deteriorate. Jeannie always pointed a finger at the BBC television programme *That Was the Week That Was* as a turning point of contemporary history: it set out to destroy Establishment values by giggles, and proposed nothing in replacement.

She made the maintenance of standards the theme of her three novels. She was always secret in the writing of them. She never discussed constructional problems with me. I might, in fact, never have known she was writing a novel except for her periodic absence in her studio hut. Some writers are impelled to share their day's writing. Jeannie never did. Nor do I for that matter. The novelist Howard Spring for instance, author of *Shabby Tiger, My Son, My Son*, and *Fame is the Spur*, used to hand his writing product of the day to his wife in the evening who would then type it. His writing life was orderly. Indeed, one of the attractions I had towards the writing game when I was a teenager came from stories about the manner in which established writers – Galsworthy, Walpole, Maugham – worked regular hours, then produced bestsellers. There was never any mention of outside interference: no questions of dealing with correspondence, bills, general household problems. None of these seemed to exist.

Jeannie would spend hours every day looking after the various crops, hands in the soil, undeterred by gales and drenching rain . . . and yet finding the time, and severing herself from her peasant way of life, to write a trilogy of hotel novels that mirror London's sophisticated life from the outbreak of the Second World War up to the eighties.

I was less secretive when I wrote a book. She might be halfway through a novel before she showed me what she had written. In my case I was impatient to have her support. Hence after I had completed a chapter, I would collect the pages together, then hand them to her nervously . . . and after that I would disappear, perhaps up to the bridge, puffing at my pipe, or standing there with a glass of whisky in my hand, soon emptied, while awaiting her verdict. I would look at my watch. She ought to have read it by now. Is she delaying seeing me because she doesn't want to upset me? And she thinks the chapter is no good? Sometimes she said just that, and I would argue that the passage which she particularly criticised was justified; and at other times she gave me the praise I needed from her, the surge of enthusiasm which is needed by anyone who is engaged, full of doubt, on a personal endeavour.

I acted in the same way towards her. She too, in due course, would hand her manuscript nervously to me, and I would then go off to my studio in the wood to read it. There was one occasion when I thought the last pages of a final chapter were wrong. It was a terrible moment. A friend had come from the Midlands to type her book, and she was about to start typing this last chapter when Jeannie showed it to me.

I remember the afternoon so clearly. I came out of my studio hut in the wood, and began walking back to the cottage across the donkey field, and I saw Jeannie in the distance, by the little entrance gate to the donkey field, and I knew that she was waiting there, hoping, hoping, that I would be running across the field, ecstatic in my praise. But I didn't run across the field. I walked very slowly, and so she knew my verdict before I reached her. I explained my reasons, and she did not demur. She took the manuscript from my hand, and disappeared to her own hide-out. In due course she handed me the new version. It was beautiful. The last chapter of *Bertioni's Hotel*, and the love scene in Paris, is one of the most moving I have read in any novel. A couple of years later she gave me the same kind of help. I handed her the last chapter of *The Cherry Tree* to read, and there was a page in it which she did not favour, and gave me strong reasons for doing so. I argued a little, then saw her point, and the page was changed. It was always helpful to us both to have such a partnership.

Jeannie has had all her life an irrational combination of assurance and timidity. She acted with assurance when the occasion did not concern her own personal efforts, but failed miserably when she should have been boasting her own achievements. She has always been touchingly unsure of her true worth. For instance, she regularly undervalued the quality of her drawings and her paintings; and so when someone wanted to buy one of them, she felt embarrassed and asked a price well below their true value.

'Oh I hate selling,' I have heard her say so often.

She was hopeless in fact in selling anything. There are some people who are naturally gifted in selling discarded household goods, clothes which are no longer wanted, and so on. Jeannie's sister, Barbara, is one such person. Barbara brought up her two sons on a shoestring and, for survival's sake, she had to develop the art of selling. Jeannie, however, took after her father. Her debonair father, Frank Nicol, a very successful London surveyor, found giving things away irresistible. Jeannie's mother was often appalled by news of the latest give-away, but she kept silent because she loved Frank. She had married him during the First World War when he was serving in the London Scottish. She married him during a leave from the Front; and after the honeymoon he went back to France and was gassed. This affected his health for the rest of his life, but never his spirit.

It is strange, though I suppose this happens in many a family situation, that Jeannie became a source of jealousy between her father and mother. She has always maintained her mother was horrible to her when she was young, always extolling the virtues of Barbara at the expense of Jeannie. Jeannie says she developed such an inferiority complex that when she was told she had been selected to play for the Hertfordshire lacrosse team in the county championship, she said: 'They've made a mistake . . . they mean Barbara.'

As the years went by, all this was to change, but a grit was always to remain in Jeannie's attitude to family life. And we shared this attitude. I too had had experiences, in my growing up, making me realise I was an outsider. We had, therefore, a special bond between us. We each respected our families, envied their normality, but were unable to tune in to their happy routines.

I had scaring moments when first I was introduced to Jeannie's family. I had arranged to meet Jeannie in St Albans at the bottom of a street which was lined with lime trees; and as I drove up to the appointed place, I saw this girl running towards me, and I felt wonderfully happy. Then we went to the family house Bryher Lodge where I was introduced. Disaster, almost immediately. I was sitting down, a small table beside me upon which was my cup of tea, when a Blue Persian cat called Tim, as I learnt later, jumped on my lap. I hated cats at that time, and I made a movement to chuck him off me – and in so doing I knocked the small table, and the contents of my tea cup spattered on the carpet.

My future mother-in-law looked severe.

My future father-in-law said, 'Have a large whisky!'

There were further mother-in-law problems when, after we had married, after our home at the finishing post of the Boat Race at Mortlake had been bombed on the occasion of our first wedding anniversary, we stayed, until the repairs were made, with Jeannie's parents at St Albans.

Obviously, because of the jobs we were doing, we often returned late to St Albans; and next morning we were greeted with frozen looks at breakfast – though a twinkle always lurked in Frank Nicol's eye.

There was, at this time, also a cat evacuee: Monty of *A Cat in the Window*. There were unfortunate occasions when Jeannie and I arrived back so late that we found ourselves in a dilemma. We had no key. We did not dare try to wake up her parents. It was then that I would go round into the garden, climb up a wall into a back window. Sometimes when I reached the window, I met Monty coming out.

But, as I have said, all this was to change as the years went by. My mother-in-law was to tell me that she suspected my motives towards her daughter after she had read my first book *Time Was Mine*, a story of my journey round the world and denounced, incidentally, from the pulpit by the vicar of our home church near Newquay, much to my father's amusement.

It was to change because Jeannie's mother came to realise that although I may not have measured up to her conception of the steady, reliable person that Jeannie should have married, I did have merits. I did not belong to her world, just as Jeannie did not belong, but she recognised that Jeannie and I belonged to each other.

I cannot remember the exact time when my relationship began to mellow. Frank Nicol died, and she came to stay with us, for five weeks or more. It was an awesome period because our cottage is not suited for prolonged stayers. In this case there was the added complication of coping with her sorrow. Unless one has experienced deep sorrow oneself, it is difficult to understand. I am sure, during those first weeks of her stay, that I may have sometimes reacted impatiently. Yet, as her stay with us continued, and she was at a loss to know where to go next, it dawned on me that here was someone so vulnerable, so hurt by memories, that it would be like kicking an injured animal, if I were to display my impatience.

The thaw in our relationship had therefore begun. I had learnt enough that there was no guile in her character, and that her integrity was intact. I learnt too that her attitude towards Jeannie and Barbara was quite impartial. 'Barbara has always been outgoing,' she said to me one evening. 'Jean has always been the inward-thinking one.'

After leaving us that time, she was to come back every Christmas, and on many other occasions; and each occasion was a happier one. I dedicated *A Cat in the Window* to her; and in *Lama*, the story of three Christmases at Minack, I wrote of her arriving at the cottage:

I watched the Land Rover splash through Monty's Leap and come up the last stretch of the lane past the stables, then round the steep piece to the right, and pull up in front of the window through which I was watching. The new coat, the new hat. I saw in the instant of watching that here again I was witnessing the wish to please. Not to be thought casual. An effort made, much thought before the choice was finally decided upon. Another Christmas, and yet seemingly no gap since the last one.

Gaily wrapped parcels in the well of the Land Rover. Just the same as it always has been.

Barbara, younger by two years, very pretty like her sister, was a bubbly girl; and within half an hour of Jeannie introducing me to her she said, 'I wish I'd met him first!' It was my first experience of her perennial wish to make people happy. Her remark was intended to make Jeannie happy by showing that she approved of me. I have never allowed her to forget it.

She was a secretary at ENSA at the time, the Services Entertainment organisation, then later she was sent to Cairo where she married Jimmy Bauer. After the war they settled in the Midlands where he was a brewer, had two sons, and then, when the sons were in their early teens, Jimmy Bauer died. Then it was that Barbara, sadly poor, set out to finance her sons during their schooling; and she did so with great dignity. She is now married to Richard Bamford, an engineering name famous throughout the world, and she still lives in the Midlands. She also continues to try to make people happy, and she embroils herself in a multitude of activities, apart from entertaining all her friends, her sons and their families. Her habit has been to write a weekly letter to Jeannie detailing an account of the previous week's engagements. Sometimes Jeannie has passed the letter on to me. 'Golly,' I would say, having read the first two pages, 'I feel tired out. I want to go to bed.'

All this was so different from Jeannie. Jeannie admired her sister for her selflessness, for the marvellous way she could wake up lethargic people and make them help those less fortunate around them. Barbara was a leader, and people warmed to her leadership. Like Jeannie, she had no sense of fear. Nothing and no one could block her from attaining her objectives.

They had therefore much in common and though, in a public way, Jeannie achieved some fame, Barbara, in a less public way, was making a similar success of her life. But it was not the life that Jeannie could ever have led. The life that Jeannie led had a different language. The same had happened to me.

I loved my family in my growing up years but became increasingly frustrated by the claustrophobic quality of the kind of life I was leading; and by the rigid, conventional, expected standard of behaviour. It was not until I went to Manchester and became a junior reporter on the *Daily Express* in their office building in Ancoats Street that I felt as suddenly free as a caged bird whose cage had been left open. Here were colleagues who were tolerant! Who understood if I made a fool of myself, and didn't make objections, sympathised even! Who had a large-screen view of life yet were sensitive to the details! Who were sophisticated, who did not shout me down if I expressed a point of view with which they disagreed! When I was in Manchester, I felt like a swallow beginning a long journey.

So too felt Jeannie when she started her career in London. She had felt curbed in her family life in St Albans. She first went to St Albans High School, then spent five years at a boarding school in Westgate, the seaside town near Margate. It was here that her talents were first nurtured, her quickness of mind, her natural gift for drawing, and the teachers were never forgotten by her. I have always believed that a sadness of the teaching profession is that the teacher is seldom aware how he or she has influenced a pupil. A teacher's achievement is anonymous. In Jeannie's case, Jeannie sought out and found the teacher who had the greatest influence on her adult life; her name was Miss Bunche, and she came to Minack once, and Jeannie was able to

31

tell her of her debt. Jeannie believed in remembering those who had helped. Mona was another, who still lives in St Albans. Mona was a servant in the Nicol household at Bryher Lodge who, believe it or not, was expected back in her room in the house on her evening off by ten thirty . . . and thus she missed the end of a movie she might be watching.

'We don't want Mona to have any followers' was the Nicol parental view, typical of that period of domestic history. About the same period, my own family would be sitting in our drawing room in the house at Newquay in Cornwall, and someone would say that more coal was needed on the fire. A bell would be pressed, and a few minutes later Anna, the maid, would appear. 'Anna,' someone would say, 'the fire needs making up.'

Jeannie loved Mona, and they have always been in touch with each other. Mona still lives in St Albans, and not far away from Mona lives another who worked in Bryher Lodge, Mary Exerxes. Jeannie, as she moved from St Albans to London, to the sophisticated world to which she effortlessly belonged, never forgot those, who, at a crucial period, helped her on her way.

Jeannie and I were destined for each other, or so it seems. There were a series of tenuous links which logical minds might explain away as being coincidences. They began early on in our lives. My father used to rent out our family home of Glendorgal near Newquay during the summer season. He was always having a perpetual battle to find the money for our education; and one summer, having rented out our splendid home on the edge of Porth cliffs, views facing up the coast towards Trevose, he rented a small up and down house for the family opposite Newquay golf course, opposite also the field where Cornish wrestling took place. Years later I was to learn that Jeannie's father rented the same house, and that Jeannie learnt to swim in Newquay harbour.

A more tenuous connection concerned Jeannie's headmistress at her Westgate boarding school. Her name was Miss Weber. I was later to discover that her brother was the headmaster of the language school in Bonn where my brother Colin went.

Jeannie's father took a special liking to a house in Bushey Heath, in a road called The Ruts; and the house itself, built in Regency times, was called Rutlands. Whenever he was in the area he always insisted on going along The Ruts and looking at the house he so loved to own.

One afternoon, at the end of a July, Jeannie was with him; and she was to tell me that she remembered clearly seeing the disconsolate figure of a young teenage boy, standing at the entrance gate of the house. It could have been me, almost certainly was me. My aunt lived at Rutlands and, at term endings from Harrow, I was parked on her pending despatch to the chosen summer holiday playground. I was lonely when I went to Rutlands. I would hang around The Ruts hoping that someone might come along who would become my friend. Not someone who might be my wife.

Jeannie's first job in London was in an office which supplied a feature to the *Daily Mirror*, a lovelorn feature. It was called the Dorothy Dix column, and Jeannie obtained the job because of the enthusiasm she showed for the newspaper world when she was interviewed. However her experience for answering the lovelorn was limited, and after a few weeks she was fired. At the same time I also was writing for the *Daily Mirror*.

'As I walked forlornly towards the Underground station,' she wrote in *Meet Me at the Savoy*, 'a number 19 bus drew up at the traffic lights. A banner along its side screamed, "Read Derek Tangye's brilliant Personality Parade in the *Daily Mirror*". I had never met him, but I recognised the two-foot high face that beamed down on me, and I glared back. To my mind he was grossly over-publicised. Five years later we were married.'

I have always been fearful of fortune tellers, avoided them. Partly this was due to my mother being told when she was very young that she would die in her fortieth year; and all through that year she was apprehensive. And she didn't die. I therefore decided that I would never seek out a fortune teller.

But I did yield on one occasion. I was on a Japanese cargo boat sailing up the Australian coast on my way to the Philippines, and one of the half dozen passengers was an English engineer going to take up an appointment in Hong Kong. He explained to me that he had studied the art of hand reading under the tuition of a famous fortune teller of the time called Cheiro. After dinner one night, my mind blunted by a full moon which lit the deck, caressing the sea in a dancing light, I yielded to his persuasion and held out my hand.

'You are going to marry a girl,' he said, 'small and dark . . . and her initials will be J.E.'

At the first dinner date I had with Jeannie, after brashly asking her to put *Time Was Mine* on the Savoy bookstall, she told me that her full name was Jean Everald Nicol. I immediately excused myself, rang up my best friend, told him that I was having dinner with the girl I was going to marry.

It seems to me yesterday.

Jeannie, on the other hand, was partial to fortune tellers. Too partial, and too superstitious, I always thought. Whenever there was a new moon I had to warn her, because she believed disaster would befall her if she first saw the new moon through glass; and having been warned by me, she would go outside the cottage, and perform a ritual of bowing, and turning round in a circle; and the performance of this ritual provided her with the confidence that all would be well in the coming months. Only by chance did I discover, a few years ago, why she sought this confidence. I discovered it by a slip of the tongue on her part, and instinctively knew that I must never disclose what I knew. Indeed I forgot about it. I had no need to remember it until this year; and then I still kept my knowledge from her, and from everyone else. I will continue to keep it to myself till later.

Propinquity is the easiest route for a love affair. As the Publicity Officer of the Savoy Hotel, she knew all the people I wanted to know in my capacity as an MI5 officer responsible for reporting weekly to the Secretary of the Cabinet. My task, among many others, was to report the gossip and the mood of influential people. I therefore began to see her often for practical reasons, making use of her in fact. Then, as my diary shows, she began to invade my thoughts, my desires; and she had a voice which bewitched me. I would ring her up and ask her to talk, talk about anything, just so that I could listen to her voice.

Diaries can be misleading. Emotional moments are written down. Diaries are a form of private confessional. Diaries can provide a backbone to one's life. A diary can prove that your true self has a reason for being content. But what you have written in your diary can only be interpreted by yourself not by a stranger.

Here are some of my diary comments during the time I first met Jeannie at the Savoy:

23 October

Jean is a gentle love. She is not worldly and sharp like the others. Her ways are without guile

. . . though, because she is moving increasingly in a world that is of a rough kind, and because she has such an influential job, she is becoming increasingly tough, and therefore more attractive. She is deliciously slim and supple, and always there to be sweet to me and love me, and she has shown me that a love affair does not always have to be noisy. Often I treat her badly but that is because I am shy of her sweetness of character, and I am running away from it.

24 October

I was low, fed up and lonely, and I wanted Jeannie to spend the evening with me, and I told her that I wanted her. But she had to see a sick girl friend and she said: 'Oh Derek, I feel I've let you down . . . you know if I had a date with a man, I would put him off.'

30 November

I'm leading a much more regulated life thanks to Jeannie. I think the girl is a saint . . . I think it would be impossible for her to say or do an unkind thing to anybody, and yet she has a lot of character. She has a fearless sort of way of looking into your eyes; a sort of shining truth. Daily I discover greater depth in her, and an astonishing wideness of reading. She can quote any lovely line which has taken her fancy. She is very clever, and it is only because she has led such a sheltered life that her conversational powers have been slim. She loves me, I think, and she is quick to learn in the ways of love.

A few weeks later.

Jeannie has changed so much, so quickly. Although she was very physically attractive and very sweet natured, I thought her a bit dull. Now I never know what funny thing is coming out of her mouth from one moment to the next. She is getting her confidence. She has changed her hairstyle which makes her look infinitely prettier. And so I am a very, very lucky person to have such a wartime love affair. When I got Howard Spring's lovely contribution for *Went the Day Well* she cried: 'I'm so happy for you!', and then yesterday she said: 'All my happiness is that you should be proud of me.' My life has been completely transformed by her.

A year later.

I'm in complete harmony with Jeannie. She is clever, sensitive, provocative, liked by all, and her love is a thing that a man may find once in a lifetime. If I married her, we would be as happy as any two people could be. She has such courage. She overcomes all sorts of home difficulties and complications in order to live with me, and because I am her man I think she would sacrifice herself in order to save me if it was necessary. She's got a delicious sense of humour, an ever-increasing knowledge of politics, a wonderful intuition, and this remarkably important job at the Savoy. What is it therefore that stops me from asking her to marry me? My unwillingness, I think, to shut the door on frivolous affairs, sudden, temporary romances which don't mean anything except their passing novelty. The fact, also, that I have never wanted to be dependent on the love of one girl. Selfishness, of course. Yet I have these great surges of love for Jeannie, and I know that she would give me the world if she could. What stops me? I suppose it is because deep down I realise I am a curiously complete person, the sort of person who can survive loneliness, never any craving for company. But I love the girl, and it far outweighs my other feelings. She is unique. I will never find anyone like her for the rest of my life. I am on the verge of asking her. I feel the decision will be made soon.

12 January

We're engaged!

20 January

I'm ecstatically happy at the thought of being married to my darling Jeannie. I have so fallen in love with her that I could not be happier. All the wonderful years ahead of us if we can surive this war. Her parents were at first horrified, and refused to give us their blessing! But they have come round, her father at any rate. He drenched me with champagne at El Vino's yesterday, after I had very formally asked him for the hand of his daughter.

But how she has been welcomed by my own family! My mother adores her. She said to me that she felt as if she was a friend of her own generation. That meant of course that Jeannie is so mature that age difference means nothing. It is a question of being on the same wavelength.

I was reminding Jeannie today of the first time she met my mother and father. 'Beakers' Penrose had lent us his house Lambe Creek on the Fal river near Truro, and it was our first holiday away together. At the end of a few days I took Jeannie to stay for a night with my parents before going back to London. My father had rented Glendorgal to a rich man for the war duration, and he and my mother were living at Cavern Cottage, beside a steep hill rising out of Porth Bay near Newquay. The cottage was cramped. I had to sleep on the sofa.

After that wonderful holiday, I gave Jeannie a special copy of *Time Was Mine*. I wrote in it an inscription to remind us both of the first holiday together:

> So to remember Wild Wood
> the swans of Lambe Creek;
> Ernie;
> The rowing boat across the Fal at Malpas;
> And one morning in a gale on the cliffs of
> Trevelgue.

28th February

We were married on the 20th at 12.15 p.m. in the little chapel nearest the main chapel in Richmond Parish Church. Just the families were there, Colin best man, Ronald the usher, Nigel, Dorothy Bailey supporting my mother. Mother had come up several days before because we both wanted her with us because she would be, we knew, so helpful in a practical way. But the poor darling had a terrible cold and had to stay in bed most of the time. She was so worried that she was being a nuisance, but she was never a nuisance. She listened patiently to all our problems, gave us sympathy and enthusiasm. Never failed us.

The service was performed by the Reverend

Harold Gray. It was very short, and as Jeannie came into the church with her father the organist performed an imperfect rendering of 'Jerusalem'; and as she came down the aisle Colin whispered to me, 'Give her a smile!'

Then afterwards, Jeannie looking so lovely in her white wedding dress, wearing the Earl of Dudley veil which Patricia Ward had arranged with the Dudley family to lend her, we had a great party at Cholmondeley House. A wonderful party of friends from every section of the world we knew. Alas, I drank too much champagne.

We went to Brighton for our honeymoon, staying at the Royal Crescent on the front. Everyone recognised Jeannie because her picture was in all the papers, and strangers were coming up to wish her happiness ... I said to someone who congratulated us: 'Yes, I'm very lucky. I have a wife who has all the virtues ... and all the provocative qualities.'

17 March

Does everyone believe when they marry that their marriage will last for ever and ever?

Jeannie and I believe so ... but we are, of course, both romantics.

Well, we have been married many years; and now on this January evening, in the home where our roots lie deep, I was confessing to her that I had been ruminating, just ruminating.

FOUR

'Derek,' said Jeannie, 'here I've been on my hands and knees picking up the drawing pins all this time while you were supposed to be giving comfort to Merlin, and you've done nothing about it. Just ruminating.'

'I'm going to see him now, straightaway.'

'Then I'll come with you.'

'That would be lovely.'

It sounds a banal remark. I have often thought how remarks, sentences, comments, which were once considered so fresh and original, have now been labelled banal or trite. Yet if they are uttered sincerely, they can still be fresh and original. So it was lovely for Jeannie to come with me to see Merlin.

Jeannie wrapped herself up in a coat which she kept for stormy weather, and I took a torch, and we went down to the stable field where I swung the torch around, but saw no Merlin. Then we went up through the gap into the QE2 field, so called because Captain Warwick, the first captain of the QE2, expressed a wish to visit Minack, but added that he would have to bring the QE2 along with him. She arrived punctually, as arranged, at 5 p.m. one summer's day. Penny and Fred hooted a greeting. The QE2, a mile off-shore, sounded her sirens in reply. Geoffrey, a true Cornishman, who worked for us at the time remarked: 'This will make a good wreck.'

Jeannie and I walked up through the gap, and once again I swung my torch to and fro, like a wartime search-light scouring for a marauding enemy bomber. The field was still dormant of bulbs, no hint of their green spikes. Soon, however, within three weeks perhaps, the spikes would begin to show: varieties like Hollywood, Dutchmaster, Magnificence and Joseph MacLeod. Once upon a time, when we invested our money in them, these varieties were fashionable, and fetched good prices. How excited Jeannie and I were when we bought them, planted them, rejoiced in the first harvest. If there is a brief period when daffodils are scarce, due to the wea-ther or some strike, they can still fetch a fair price. But they no longer provide the hopeful glint in our eyes as when we first bought them. More often they are not worth the expense of picking them. So we leave them to decorate the QE2 field as a carnival of flowers.

'Where *can* he be?'

'I can see a white nose!' said Jeannie.

He was standing at the top of the field beneath a section of the hedge which was as high as a may tree. Other sections of this particular hedge were much lower; and this sometimes caused problems. Young steers belonging to our friend Jack Cockram, hungry for new pastures, would, on occasions, breach the lower part of the hedge and career into the QE2 field, and beyond. They terrified Merlin, and he would race away from them in a panic. Fred, however, used to face them with the courage of a stag at bay. Fred would bellow defiance at them. Not Merlin. Poor Merlin had little to bellow with. He was a silent donkey – until a moment about which I will tell.

Cherry suffered in the same way. True she had a concert-sized purr, but she was unable to make any normal cat noise. She could not, for instance, miaow, or make that rasping, cackling noise which many cats like to make when they are demanding food from those who cater for their changeable appetites. All Cherry could do, except for the purr, was a tiny squeak; and you had to bend down close to her to hear it.

This weakness in her noise machine posed a worry in our minds. Supposing she fell into some cavity from which she was unable to get out? Supposing she was up in a tree and could not get down? Supposing, in a period of snow, she became trapped in a snow drift? All the usual kinds of worries which envelope anyone who loves.

There came a night when our imaginary worries became a reality.

It was three weeks before Christmas. At eight o'clock on the particular evening, I went into the spare room expecting to see Cherry spreadeagled on the night storage heater which Jeannie called the Heat-purr. It had a teak top, and this was pleasant for Cherry: she was like a holidaymaker lying on a sunny beach. On this occasion there was no sign of her.

The entrance into the spare room is carved out of the massive end wall of the cottage. It was a great occasion when we decided that this was to be done. We had already bought a chicken house and converted it, adjacent to the cottage, into a living room where Jeannie was to write *Meet Me at the Savoy*, and where we used to bunch our Bournemouth Gem violets for market; and we were soon to add a bathroom at the far end. But there was no contact with the cottage, and so, if we wanted a bath, we had to walk outside to reach it.

This belonged to the innocent, pioneer days when such inconveniences did not matter. The joy of each day lay in the freedom we relished. Not just the freedom of being on one's own, but the freedom of being without the conventional necessities that society considers to be of such fundamental importance.

Walking in the rain to our bathroom, at the time, seemed to be part of the happiness that we were living.

Nonetheless we succumbed, in due course, to more logical behaviour. A door-sized hole was carved out of the end wall, and a wood-covered doorway created which enabled us to walk to the spare room, walk to the bathroom, without an umbrella or a mackintosh.

The first person who experienced this luxury was my mother who came to stay with us soon after the work had been completed.

My mother, an unswerving supporter of our adventure from the beginning, appeared on her first evening, elegant in evening dress, pausing at the new entrance between one time chicken house and cottage, saying 'Oh my dears, I'm so glad for you. Now you've got everything.'

I remember how Jeannie and I so agreed with her, and Jeannie saying joyously: 'Yes, we've now got everything!'

We had no electricity.

No fridge.

No freezer.

No dishwasher.

No washing machine.

No vacuum cleaner.

Lighting was by candles and paraffin lamps.

I returned to the spare room around ten o'clock, and there was still no sign of Cherry. I was alarmed. It was so out of character. It was her habit always to be indoors when night fell.

'I'm going out to look for her,' I said to Jeannie as I looked for the torch.

I looked everywhere, called everywhere, opened the greenhouse doors, opened the door of the cat's kitchen, the little hut where we used to bunch daffodils, now the site of a calor-gas stove where the stinking fish is poached. No sign of Cherry. I walked up to the field where the California daffodils grow. I walked up the lane, across Monty's Leap. I opened the door of my office which is part of the stable building, an office which I call my confusion room because there is so much in this room which I intend to deal with . . . many things put there because we didn't know where else to put them, boxes of photographs, boxes of magazines . . . all of which I put off to another day, yet another day. I had switched on the light. No sign of Cherry.

I had now begun to panic. She had been caught by a fox. She had been drowned in the small reservoir. Perhaps a stoat had attacked her, or a mink! Minks were running wild in west Cornwall, and only a few days before I had been told that they were killing any small animal they could find, including cats. Cherry was gone. I would never see her again.

It was time to return to Jeannie.

She was sitting, curled in her chair in front of the fire, perusing the *Oxford Book of Quotations*, the copy that my mother gave her once as a Christmas present.

'Darling,' I cried, 'Cherry has gone, vanished. We're never going to see her again!'

Jeannie continued to peruse the *Oxford Book of Quotations*.

'Jeannie!' I cried out again, my voice in anguish, 'Cherry has gone! We're never going to see her again! Don't you feel as I do about her?'

Jeannie looked up at me, the book on her lap.

'You're over-excited. Cherry has got something on her mind, and does not wish to be disturbed. Or, if she is trapped somewhere, go round very quietly and you'll hear that squeak,' and then she added, 'if you don't find her in the next half hour, then I'll join you – but I think you will have found her.'

45

And I did.

I made my search rounds again, and once more went into my confusion room. I switched on the light, stood still, listened . . . and heard a squeak.

Cherry had managed to reach a high top shelf – and couldn't get down. Shouts of delight from me. Absurd how happy I felt. There she was peeping down at me and, saying in thought, that she was in a predicament and depended upon me to solve it. I of course proceeded to do so, and fetched a ladder, climbed up it, grasped Cherry in my arms, and descended. Just as I reached the bottom rung, Cherry struggled, and in a second she was flying through the air, then landed in the box where Jeannie had placed the Christmas tree decorations, breaking many of the baubles.

So Cherry's squeak served its purpose, and brought relief and much happiness. Merlin, on the other hand, when at last he made his first hee-haw was at a moment of sadness; and a moment which proves that an animal can experience anguish as a human being can.

Jeannie was standing beside him that day when Fred was being taken away from the stable to Oliver land where he was to be buried, standing on ground above the cottage where she could see the winding lane. Jack Cockram and Walter Grose had taken charge of the situation, and they intuitively understood that I would not want to be too much involved in the details. They were going up the lane in the tractor, slowly, Jack driving, Walter walking beside it, his cap off, carrying it in respect, as if he was acknowledging Fred, whom he had known since he was born, as a personal friend; and there was Jeannie, Merlin beside her, the sweep of Mount's Bay with its beauty, its history before her, and the little cortège of Fred going its way, when there was a heartrending hee-haw from Merlin. He stood shivering, crying out his anguish that his old friend had gone away. At last, Merlin had found his hee-haw.

The white nose in the dark now moved across the field to meet us; and when it came close, nuzzling Jeannie, she put out a hand to touch it.

'Merlin,' she said. 'we've brought you some carrots.'

Her arm went round his shaggy neck, hugging him, while I fumbled in my pocket for the carrots, carrots I had sliced from end to end, because I have always been scared by stories that whole carrots can block a donkey's throat, stopping it from swallowing, choking it.

For a few minutes we murmured sweet nothings to him, then turned to go back to the cottage, and he proceeded to follow us, came right up to the gate where we said goodnight to him, again murmuring sweet nothings.

'You know,' said Jeannie when we were back in the cottage, and I was sitting in my corner of the sofa and Jeannie was in her chair in front of the fire, the open fire, set beneath the age-old granite lintel, 'tonight I feel mortal.'

I looked across at her, and laughed.

'You certainly don't look it,' I said.

Jeannie has always been ageless. On the day of her twenty-first birthday, celebrating it at a hotel on the Isles of Scilly, a lady guest said crossly: 'The girl is not twenty-one, more like fourteen. Her parents are very wrong in letting her pretend that she is older than she is.'

Then there have been several occasions when we have been in some public place and someone has come up to me and asked: 'Tell me, what does your pretty daughter do?'

Such questions amused me. There was not all that

age difference between us, but it so happened that Jeannie seemed to possess the gift of eternal youth.

Her height was five feet five inches. She was slim like a boy. Her hands were slender, her fingers tapered. Her eyes changed colour according to what she was wearing, from grey-blue to green. Her hair, shoulder-length, was dark, and although she complained that it was too fine, making trouble for her hairdresser, it possessed a casual elegance. It always remained dark: no outside help was ever needed. There was her smile. She believed that most people are fundamentally vulnerable, and that they require to be given confidence; and whenever strangers appeared at Minack, there would be this smile. She put herself in their place. She too was vulnerable. She had been through the same experience. She was aware of the emotional struggle when one has a yearning to meet someone one had never met. A yearning, not in the category of seeing a television or movie character, but someone who makes you feel they share the same wavelength. If a stranger, a reader of the story, arrived, Jeannie gave a welcome because she was utterly natural. She was as interested in the stranger as the stranger was interested to meet Jeannie. There was a perennial spring blossom about Jeannie. Minds danced when they met her.

'Why do you say you feel mortal?' I asked. 'You're not hiding anything from me?'

'Of course not. I've never felt better. It's Fred who has upset me and made me feel mortal. It's only yesterday that I carried him into the barn, Penny following me, and I suddenly realise time is going by. Silly, I know, but I didn't think death belonged to us. At this moment I realise it does.'

I found it strange she should speak in this way because she was one of the war generation of pretty girls who lived daily with death. Bombs on cities killed them. Lovers, temporary, permanent, casual, were every day reported missing. These girls had a role to play, providing a thrill, or offering a man in great danger an illusion of love, or acting as an anchor for the man to go back to, one leave after another; and long after one of the pretty girls had forgotten a man, he was remembering her. These pretty girls of Jeannie's generation were often confused. It was not easy for them to find the dividing line between having fun for themselves and consoling those who might soon be killed.

Jeannie knew too many of her generation who were killed; and I believe that one reason why she gave up her hugely successful job with its glamour and frivolous pleasures was because she was haunted by memories of those who died in the war. She felt that the peace was being lost, and so many had died in vain. They had died innocently, believing they were helping to preserve the small green fields of Britain, the traditions, law and order, integrity as a way of life; and always the sanctity of the homes and the streets they left. Intuitively she now knew that her destiny lay elsewhere. She had had her fun in London's sophisticated world; and it would now be like a tape being endlessly repeated. We both were ready for the change. We both were ready to live at Minack without running water, electricity, and on only £3 a week.

'What do we do about Merlin?' I asked.

'About getting a companion, you mean?'

'Yes.'

We had the same attitude towards such a situation. We were loth to acquire a replacement for a pet speedily. We believed in fate solving the problem. A speedy replacement seemed an indulgence that betrayed years of love. There is also another very different attitude which is sensible. Quickly fill the vacancy, and you have given an unwanted cat or dog a home.

In our case, however, we had become accustomed to fate solving the problem. Lama, out of the wild, had replaced Monty; Oliver and Ambrose had replaced Lama; Cherry also had arrived out of nowhere. And we acquired Penny and Fred only because we happened to have a good time at the Plume of Feathers pub.

'We have to wait,' said Jeannie. 'I couldn't bear the thought at this time to go out looking for another donkey.' Then she added, smiling: 'It's not that Merlin will be alone during the summer. He'll get lots of attention just because he is on his own.'

There was also his interest in Nellie, the grey donkey belonging to the farm which at one point borders the land near the Ambrose Rock in Oliver land. Nellie, successor to Duncan who had died and who had been a friend both of Penny and Fred, would sometimes appear in the field divided by a stone hedge where Merlin grazed. He had quickly become besotted by her; and the previous summer, Fred's last summer, Fred would watch with tolerant amusement as Merlin careered across the land in order to be close to his Nellie. It was a frustrating affair. Nellie was a tease: she wasn't really interested. Nonetheless, another summer of frustration would help to occupy Merlin, and take his mind off being on his own.

'Mind you,' I said, 'if someone walks down the lane with a donkey I wouldn't turn it away, and nor would you.'

'Of course not.'

'It is just that at this particular period we don't want to force a decision.'

'Exactly.'

Meanwhile there was a form of guerrilla warfare in

progress between Ambrose and Cherry; and we had the task of being the umpires.

It was understandable that Ambrose took objection to Cherry. She had arrived on the scene from nowhere, thus intriguing us; and had now become, to the dismay of Ambrose, tenderly loved by us both. She was very pretty, and the spattered apricot colours on her black fur gave her a style. Ambrose, beautiful Ambrose, was bewildered as to how to deal with the situation. For so long the undisputed King of Minack, he was now faced with an unwanted Queen.

His tactics were puzzling. For instance, there was a sharp difference between his behaviour towards her indoors and his behaviour towards her outdoors.

Indoors there was a demarkation line between the sitting room and the spare room. Cherry, after using the corner behind my desk for a bedroom, decided that the spare room would be the ideal home for her. Every night she would retire there; and every day she would go there when she wanted to rest undisturbed. Thus the spare room became Cherry's room.

Ambrose was understandably disturbed by this because he too enjoyed retiring to the spare room; and he used to lie on the bed beneath a painting by Jeannie of Monty. It was uncanny, looking first at the painting, then Ambrose beneath it, because both appeared to be identical.

Ambrose, up to a point, accepted Cherry's takeover of the spare room. He would come to the entrance and stop there, pouting, obviously annoyed but not annoyed enough to make a row. It was the same when mealtimes came. Mealtimes, of course, always seem to come frequently; and the opening of a tin, the bending, the picking up of a dirty plate, the discarding of a saucer of milk, the turn-away nose at something you thought would be a delicacy – such episodes are well known to those who have cats. In Cherry's case, however, she was more amenable, certainly more amenable than Ambrose. Thus, if Ambrose turned up his nose on some delicacy, Cherry would approach his plate, and devour its contents. What was so strange was that Ambrose showed no objection. Sphinx-like, he would watch her, enjoying herself.

Outside, in the area around Minack, there was a different mood.

Jeannie had a dream that one day we would walk down the lane, walk even to the Ambrose Rock, with Ambrose and Cherry in harmonious companionship, just as Oliver and Ambrose used to walk with us.

Unhappily Ambrose's attitude outside the cottage was of uncontrollable fury towards Cherry. Jeannie and I might set off on a walk, Cherry joyfully beside us, when Ambrose suddenly saw what was happening, and go for Cherry like a bullet. Cherry was very quick. I never saw them meet in a collision. But Ambrose was making it clear to us all that although he would tolerate Cherry indoors, he was not going to allow her peacefully to enjoy the area outside which he considered his personal territory.

I should not, however, give the impression that all was permanently peaceful indoors; and that was mainly the fault of Cherry.

Cherry, on seeing Ambrose near her, would emit a tiny rasping noise, the sound of a toy tin trumpet, and would even shoot out a paw. It was, I feel sure, a gesture of fear. Ambrose, great, beefy Ambrose, must have appeared a terrible threat to her. One swipe of his paw and he could knock her out in the first round. Yet Ambrose never showed any intention, indoors, of using that paw. He would look at her sedately as she made her tin-trumpet noise, as if he was saying to himself what a foolish little thing she was.

This situation with two cats who did not love each other obviously upset Jeannie and me; and we had the tricky game of balancing our own love for them both. Ambrose as the senior, someone who had shared so many of our struggles, our failures and our successes, naturally required priority because he belonged over the years to Minack. Cherry, on the other hand, every day entering more deeply into our hearts, also deserved special attention. She adored being at Minack. We were the only people in her life to whom she could give her love. We were in a quandary. The old, old story when one loves two people.

'Tell you what we'll do,' said Jeannie one day.

'Yes?'

'It's night time when Cherry feels most vulnerable. There she is alone in the spare room while Ambrose is purring away on our bed.'

'Yes?'

'I therefore suggest that if one of us wakes up during the night and can't get to sleep again, we go to the spare room and settle in the bed for a while. Cherry will then feel fussed over.'

I looked at her in astonishment. She may have converted me into being a cat lover, but not to that extent.

'I think you're potty,' I said. 'Nothing, nothing will make me leave a warm bed to give company to a cat.'

FIVE

The daffodil harvest was late, the year that Fred died.
Jeannie picked the first daffodils on 2 February, and
we usually begin sending away in the third week of
January. This lateness threatened a poor season because early growers in the far west of Cornwall had to
sell their daffodils before the factory-type growers
began to send daffodils to the markets. Our own slow
method of picking in small meadows, close to the sea
cannot compete in commercial terms with these big
growers. They score over us in another way. They are
not primarily concerned, like ourselves, in selling
daffodils in bloom. Their main interest is selling the
bulbs. Hence, for such people, earnings from daffodils
provide a bonus – but in achieving this they swamp
the markets and bring the prices down.

On 8 February we sent our first two boxes away to
New Covent Garden Market. They were of the
Magnificence variety, a yellow trumpet with a faint
scent, and there were sixty bunches in each box. We
had picked them in the bottom meadows of the Merlin
cliff, three baskets of them, and it meant a long clamber
back, me with two baskets, Jeannie with one; and when
we reached the top Jeannie said: 'We must be fit doing
this without puffing!'

We were primarily doing this work for the sake of
pride. We were the last of the daffodil cliff growers

between Penzance and Gwennap Head, near Land's End. Every other grower had given up because prices did not compensate for the cost of labour. Yet Jeannie had this passion to continue. It was perhaps an echo of her childhood which would prompt her to say to me, me tired and ready for a rest, 'I'm going out to pick the Obs down the cliff!' An echo because, when she was a child, there was a legendary captain of the steamship *Scillonian* which sailed between Penzance and the Scilly Islands called Captain Reseigh. He sailed the *Scillonian* in such ferocious weather that even today, if the modern *Scillonian* stays in harbour when the weather is bad, a local will comment: 'Captain Reseigh wouldn't have feared the weather.'

It was the same mood of pride that reflected Jeannie's wish to pick the daffodils in the cliff meadows.

'I don't want, after all these years,' she said that spring, 'passengers in the *Scillonian* passing by and seeing that we have left our meadows to go wild like the rest. I don't want them to think we've surrendered to modern commercial pressures.'

Dear Jeannie, I so often have had to talk to her in sensible fashion, bringing her dreams down to reality.

'But,' I said, 'I can't go on forever carrying baskets up the cliff or scything the bracken and undergrowth from the meadows every autumn, just for the sake of passengers on the *Scillonian*.'

The two boxes fetched £18 each, and we rejoiced. Within a week the price was down to £9 a box, and we were miserable. The weather had turned mild, daffodils in our fields had been encouraged to leap into market readiness. No longer could Jeannie and I cope on our own, and our helpers of past daffodil seasons, Margaret Smith and Joan Johnson, had to be enlisted; Margaret gave up riding her horse in the morning, Joan gave up her other work. Their presence was infectiously happy: both were so enthusiastic, both were as happy as we were when, at the end of the day, we had picked and bunched a record number of boxes.

But there was the cost of sending those boxes. I calculated that the cost of each box – the commission, the freight, the box itself, other items like rubber bands and the petrol taking the load to Long Rock, the other side of Penzance, the wages of Margaret and Joan, and for that matter the wages of ourselves – all this totalled more than £7 a box. There was the added complication that we never knew what price our daffodils would fetch when we sent them away. We never knew until a few days later when the postman brought us the invoice. True, we could gain a general impression of the state of the flower market from the local selling representative, but it was usually only a general impression. But sometimes he would declare, 'Don't send any more, Spalding is on. There's a glut!' On other occasions we had to discover the glut for ourselves – days later when our invoices arrived.

One of the problems surrounding the daffodil harvest is the inability to speed output. There is no machine which will career up the rows picking daffodils, no machine which will bunch them. Every step in daffodil production has to be done by hand labour. The large growers hire casual workers on piece-work rates, paying them for the number of bunches they pick and bunch in the open field. Jeannie and I have never grasped how this system can be successful. For instance, there is a gale blowing, or rain belting down, or it is very cold – yet the casual workers, most of them unaccustomed to such conditions, rubber bands in their shivering hands, are expected to operate for several hours on end.

Our method of handling the daffodil harvest was to

56

pick, then bring the daffodils to the small greenhouse where they were bunched in comfort. This also had the advantage of scanning each daffodil stem so that each one was perfect in the bunch. It is difficult to believe that the outside casual workers can be so careful.

The speed of picking doffodils depends, of course, upon the number of daffodils ready to be picked. Daffodils are not inclined to appear ready for market all at the same time. Hence we may begin to pick a meadow of Joseph MacLeod, my favourite yellow daffodil, yet, as I go up the row I find many have, on that day, stems which are still too short, and which must be left for another day. On the other hand, we have sometimes been in a meadow where all stems are ready; and then we have a joyous rush of picking. Pickers, understandably, vary in speed. Jeannie was always a champion picker, twice as fast as myself. I timed myself once. I took fifty minutes to pick 600 stems. I also timed my bunching time. I spent one hour bunching six dozen bunches, ten daffodils in each bunch. Jeannie was grateful for my help. But she was not impressed.

Yet there is an aspect of the daffodil season which never fails to give pleasure. Jeannie and I could wake up in the morning and know that we would not be embarking upon a task during the coming day which was destructive, morally or physically. Every bunch of daffodils would soon be decorating a corner of some far-away room, soothing a sensitive person, lighting up their minds, calming them, exciting them into being reminded that the basic values of happiness always remain the same. What is a basic value? Honesty is one, tolerance another, tolerance in the sense that you understand someone else's attitude though you may not agree with it. Loyalty is another basic value, and by that I mean loyalty to a belief that has stood the test of time but which is being challenged by a change of fashion. Ever-changing fashion is indeed always the challenger to basic values. Basic values can never be trendy, and so they are dull. They never come to life until a person becomes weary of deceit, endlessly repeated.

When we bunched, just ourselves alone in the first stages of the daffodil harvest, we would have an intermittent conversation.

'I was thinking,' I said, picking a handful of stems from a tin, counting one to ten, 'of the night we lost the White Leghorns.'

'What possibly makes you think of them?'

'The snowdrops, there on the bank in front of us.'

'Why them?'

'They're white, and quite irrationally my mind returned to the night we brought the White Leghorns back here.'

Memory is so confusing. Often you cannot remember what you did yesterday, or an hour before when you put your spectacles in a safe place and now cannot find them; and yet incidents, long-ago incidents, seemingly unimportant at the time, are suddenly recalled as if a torch is shining upon them.

The White Leghorns incident was, however, of only trivial importance. Heaven knows why at that moment when I looked at the snowdrops I remembered the occasion so vividly. Perhaps the reason was that we both shared it, that it was part of our haphazard growing up in the countryside; and in any case it was funny.

We had kept chickens at our home in Mortlake. Their home was a sturdily built air-raid shelter at the end of the garden; and there were a few yards of the garden, surrounded by wire netting, which gave them the chance to scratch around in comparative freedom.

Jeannie, coming home from a day at the Savoy Hotel, loved to rush up to the nesting boxes in the air-raid shelter, feeling into the straw, and finding an egg.

The chickens were Rhode Island Reds; and there was one Rhode Island Red which possessed such an aura of character that we named her Queen Mary. When we left London to begin our new life in Cornwall, we had no hesitation in taking Queen Mary and her entourage of six other Rhode Island Reds with us.

We wired in a patch of ground where the washing line now stands, on top of the slope above the cottage, and Queen Mary and her friends lived there during that first glorious summer, laying their eggs in a very small chicken house we provided for them. Queen Mary's eggs were spasmodic. She was elderly, had been with us when the bombs fell on London, but she still pottered around wanting to be useful; and so we gave her a clutch of eggs to sit upon. Out of that clutch, one egg was hatched; and the chick proved, in due course, to be a cockerel. This was too much for Queen Mary, and she waned; and there came a day when we asked the vet to put her to sleep.

When the wind and rain came that first autumn, we knew we had to change the site of the chicken run; and we moved it down to the wood in front of the cottage where there was a certain shelter from the wind and the rain. We also acquired an enlarged chicken house, and this we installed in the wood, surrounded by high wire netting dug a foot into the ground, the aim being to prevent any fox from making a raid. Into this arena were scheduled the White Leghorns . . .

We bought a dozen one late afternoon at a farm auction, put them in a wire-topped crate in the well of the Land Rover we had at the time, and arrived back at Minack when night had fallen.

The crate was too heavy for me to carry to the

entrance of our new chicken arena. The distance between where I had stopped the Land Rover and the entrance was fifty yards. Easy, we both thought, we will carry them there one by one. Unhappily, when I undid the top of the crate, the White Leghorns rushed at the comparatively small gap I had made, surprised me into panicking, surprised Jeannie too; and we suddenly found that all the twelve White Leghorns had vanished from the Land Rover into the night darkness. It was midnight before we recovered them all. The last one we found by torchlight at the top of an elm close to Monty's Leap; and I had to fetch a ladder and climb up, an arm stretched out to catch it. 'Be careful,' I heard Jeannie murmuring below me, 'do be careful.'

So we remembered this story, and fell silent again.

There are sounds at winter's end that a year's interval has made you forget; sights too, and scents. I forget that gulls' cries become urgent, more demanding. I forget the burble of a robin, silent for the previous months. I forget the sudden eruption of the blue tits, and the coal tits, flighting in branches around the cottage, expecting that I have nothing better to do than to throw sunflower seeds to them all day long. I forget the sweet scent of the heliotrope. I forget that nettles like tiny fists are growing again, that gorse is speckled with yellow petals that smell as if summer has come. I forget that the bracken in the croft land is so flat and dead that you cannot imagine it will ever be green again. I forget that there always comes a morning when the air is soft and the sun is shining, that the senses are suddenly deliciously aware of the coming of spring.

I carried on bunching.

'Jeannie,' I said, 'what would you do if I were run over by a bus?'

She was at the other end of the bench by the door. One of the cardboard flower boxes which I had stapled together was on the bench in front of her.

'Oh don't interrupt,' she said. 'I'm counting.'

'Sorry.'

She was counting the bunches she was putting in the box, and the counting required concentration. The variety she was packing was Magnificence. Fifty bunches in the box was the target.

'Yes?' she said, when she had finished. 'What were you saying?'

'Only a bit of fantasy. I was asking what you would do if I were run over by a bus.'

'You know very well what I would do. I would stay here. I will stay here for ever and for ever, I will be here when I die, my spirit will be everywhere. I will love all those who live here and love Minack, but if any philistine misuses Minack, I'll turn into a witch and haunt them! What would you do if I were run over by a bus?'

'I would be terribly unhappy.'

She laughed.

'Seriously, I mean.'

'I would become a hermit. Never move out. Welcome people yes, but I would never go away unless I had to.'

'How lucky we are to have roots.'

The box of Magnificence was packed, and she put it aside, and began packing another.

'Oddly enough,' I added, 'my only worry would be Ambrose and Merlin and Cherry. What would happen to them?'

'Oh don't let's imagine things.'

Her daffodil clothes were slacks, polo-neck jersey and anorak; and she wore gumboots. Practical but not elegant. She was wearing the same type of gear, years before, when she received a telegram from the BBC, asking her to appear on the famous *Tonight* programme. Arnold Bennett's *Imperial Palace*, the novel based on the Savoy Hotel, was being serialised on television, and Jeannie was wanted to make her comments on the production.

Within twenty-four hours, slacks, polo-neck jersey and gumboots were exchanged for Jeannie's other ego, the very sophisticated ego in a Savoy Hotel suite with windows overlooking the Thames. What was so remarkable about her was that she took the switch so naturally. She was at home there as if she was at Minack. She was intuitively sure of herself. It was easy to understand why she had never been a feminist. She didn't have to make strident noises and gestures in order to justify herself. She was innately feminine. She charmed and fascinated men, making them feel at ease and take jokey risks. Any man, be it a Danny Kaye or a George Trewhella, our Penzance butcher, who won her custom by running into the street after her first visit to his shop, calling out: 'You must be in love! You've left your change behind!'

The *Tonight* programme was on a Thursday at ten o'clock – perhaps later, I have forgotten. But the timing posed the problem as to how Jeannie would best occupy the time beforehand, and be at her most sparkling form when the programme time arrived. A good dinner in the Savoy Grill was decided upon, followed by a chauffeur-driven car to Television Centre. She was greeted ceremoniously by the producer, introduced to the interviewer who took her aside and asked a lot of questions, lulling her into thinking they would be the same questions when the programme was live . . . and then, after make-up had been applied, she was led to her seat in front of the cameras. It was now that disaster nearly befell her.

I had been following her around like a nurse, in the background but always awaiting the call of any emergency. The emergency took place a few minutes before the programme began. Jeannie started to choke, a nervous reaction to the tension that had been building up. Worse was to come. I was holding in my hand a glass containing a warm remnant of a BBC whisky. Jeannie saw it, held out her hand, took it, and swallowed it. A few seconds later she began to hiccup. British television viewers were about to see her hiccuping. A terrible moment for her.

'Then,' she said later, 'the interviewer began asking me the questions I didn't expect – and mind triumphed over matter.'

Next day she was a passenger in a Savoy lift.

'Did you see that very pretty girl,' she heard a fellow lift passenger say, 'on the *Tonight* programme talking about *Imperial Palace*?'

She hid her face.

I have always felt when waiting for Jeannie, returning to Jeannie, a feeling of excitement. There has always been so much to talk about, personal, politics, literature, music, sport. Her interests were so wide that at one moment I might be arguing with her that I believed Hardy was a more profound poet than he was a novelist; next we might be sharing the view that the boring delivery tone of a BBC woman announcer made us turn off the news broadcast, next she might tell me of a visit to a one-time hairdresser during which he asked her who was her favourite composer, and she had said Puccini – 'Madam,' said the hairdresser, 'how brave of you to admit it.' Or we might talk of sport, any sport, and the ideas we each had would be tossed between us like a tennis ball in a tennis match. Or there would be solemn moments about politics. 'Why,' I remember Jeannie saying, 'are opposition politicians and the media so blind that they don't realise the Falklands War brought freedom to Argentina? Had it not been for Mrs Thatcher and the Services the Junta would still be there, and the secret arrests would have continued.' This was the joy of being married to Jeannie. She was able to carry on a conversation about any subject, not with the dry analytical attitude of the academic mind, but with the warmth, gusto and common sense of in-born naturalness.

There was also a toughness about her character which surprised some people. The apparent sweetness would suddenly go sour when she thought she had been treated badly. A seemingly trivial incident could put her in this mood, making her appear a touchy person. The manager of a shop which she regularly attended and always paid weekly, said in a loud voice in front of many customers, 'You haven't paid your last account.' She had. She has never gone into that shop again.

At another shop she ordered a cake with which to celebrate the publication of my new book, the title of the book inscribed in icing on the top of the cake. However, I found the cake so impossible to cut, the content so cement hard, that I had to soothe her disappointment by trying to make her laugh: 'I'll go and get my chain saw.' She never went to that shop again.

We gave the cake to a fox in the end, outside an earth where five cubs were later to play. Even the fox could not cope with it. For several days we went back to see whether the cake had been consumed. No luck. A gnawing at the edges, but no more than that. At last, ten days later, Jeannie, who had gone ahead of me, called back excitedly: 'It's won approval! There are ants all over it!'

Sometimes I used Jeannie as a front, as if she were a sapper clearing a minefield. Wives are often used in this role. Wives of business executives wanting to do a deal are often used. In Jeannie's case, there was an occasion when, with her approval, I used her on the most important afternoon of our lives.

We realised at the time it *was* important, but only now do we realise *how* important. Indeed, strangers, by reading about that afternoon, long after it had happened, highlighted its importance in their letters.

One of these letters came from John Stewart Collis, the Irish writer of such wit, erudition and fluency that he will one day be recognised as the twentieth-century Jonathan Swift.

The first letter he wrote to me was the result of a radio programme Jeannie and I did; and it read as follows:

Perhaps you would agree with me that the *purest* form of communication is sometimes between strangers briefly met; and purer still if the strangers are not seen, not present.

Thus it was for me this afternoon when I heard your programme ... it moved me more than tongue can say. I could scarcely restrain my tears. These terms will seem too high; you will think it strange ... for we never know what effect, when we least expect it, we may have on others.

It was not just nostalgia on my part. I often feel that. Oh no, it was the *implications* arising from, belonging to, your utterly unstressed, un-emphasised, wonderful account ... the implications as to how humanity has lost its way. You yourselves cannot very well be aware of the combination of happiness and sadness inherent in that talk, which far transcended the story of two people.

He sent with his letter a copy of his classic *While Following the Plough*.

We became friends. He came to visit us. The three of us understood each other in subtle, unspoken ways. He was ebullient, giving me encouragement in his thrust to enjoy life while in return, I believe, Jeannie and I gave reality to the nostalgia he felt for the life he would like to have lived. He was fun to be with, far, far from being cantankerous which a reviewer of a biography of him suggested. And he had this intense intuition which normal people do not possess. A while after he first came to Minack, he wrote this letter:

I heard the last bit on Radio 4 of your book *A Donkey in the Meadow*, and it reminded me forcibly of the first time I wrote to you . . . and when, in that letter, I described to you what specially interested me. It was when you first saw the Cottage, and said to yourselves we MUST have it. But how to get it?

Everything depended upon this. Your whole life was at stake. It was an appalling crisis. The owner cared nothing about you. You had no power over him. No influence. If he refused you, all was lost. This was the crisis of your life.

There is generally some such moment in the lives of all who are people of destiny rather than victims of fate. And it is generally nothing spectacular. I have had this experience myself . . . and I have written about it in *While Following the Plough*. It was my moment of destiny, and I could not fail because it was. And you could not fail because it was your destiny.

I remember receiving his letter and not appreciating its significance. We were involved at the time in preparing the ground for planting the early potato seed. We were one-track-minded. But a few months later I picked up the letter again, during a period when we had no urgent work to do, and I perused it, and I saw that Jack Collis had expressed a feeling which I had not been able to express before. Destiny does, on occasions, take charge of one's life.

It was Jeannie, however, who realised our destiny. We had seen the cottage, nestling beside a wood, from the heap of rocks known as Carn Barges. It reached out to us, held our hands, as if it was pleading with us to realise that here lay our destiny. We were drawn towards it, an irrational pull with no logical thinking to pull us back; and we hurried along a track towards it, then crossed a field, climbed over a hedge, and there was this long-ago-built cottage, walls climbing out of rocks, a mud floor, rat droppings, a pool of rainwater in a corner, tiny windows, a wafer of a wooden wall making it appear there were two rooms – and yet exultation in both our hearts. This cottage held our destiny. How to rent it? Here the calculating side of our characters came to our help.

We found that the cottage and the land surrounding it belonged to the Lord Falmouth estates, but the property was let to a popular, buccaneer farmer called Harry Laity; who, in turn, let it, and the neighbouring farm, to what was called a dairy farmer who had no use for the cottage. So Harry Laity, it was clear, was the man to win over, to persuade that we were not passing summer visitors, fantasising about a Cornish home; and though in my first letter to him I explained that I was Cornish, that my grandfather Sir Richard Tangye was born in Broad Lane, Redruth, proving I was no outsider, I believed it would be Jeannie who would win the day, who would persuade him to let us have the cottage. A meeting was arranged.

The meeting was at his farm near Land's End called Bosistow. We took a bus from Lamorna Cove to Poljigga, a hamlet which had its moment of fame at the turn of the century. At that time there was a flourishing Glasshouse Nursery Garden known as the Vineries. The owner specialised in growing grapes. Tourists, in horse-drawn carriages and on their way to Land's End, used to call there. The quality of the grapes was famous, so famous that their fame reached Balmoral, one day in the nineties, when Queen Victoria was in residence; and at her command Poljigga grapes were despatched to her.

The decayed shell of the Vineries was still there that day Jeannie and I got off the bus, and found ourselves standing at the entrance of a lane which stretched towards Bosistow, far in the distance. It was the longest lane we have ever walked, or so it seemed; and as we walked we discussed our tactics.

'I'm going to leave it to you,' I said firmly.

'Oh Derek, you know I'm no good at being business-like.'

'I'm not asking you to be business-like.'

'Then what am I supposed to do?'

There was still a long way to walk.

'Just be feminine,' I replied, 'just be your natural self. You look so young and pretty with your long dark hair, and Harry Laity will find you irresistible. If I do the talking, his mind will switch into the way he is accustomed to talk to men – about the price of a sheep or a cow, for instance. It will be market-place talk, and I'll be out of my depth, and he'll be suspicious. What is he after, he will ask himself, am I missing out on something I don't know about?'

There we were, the two of us, walking down that long, long lane, walking towards our destiny. The farmhouse was now in sight, a granite-built farmhouse, pine trees incongruously grouped behind it.

I knew Jeannie would not fail. She had this aura of integrity and naturalness and courage. She would not appear to Harry Laity as a London butterfly trying to find a crevice where temporarily to hide; and if he did have such an impression, it would be smothered by Jeannie's enthusiasm for the life we both wanted to lead.

We arrived at Bosistow.

We were politely welcomed.

But the tactics we had devised were of no value. It was to me, to me alone, that Harry Laity's questions were directed. A question, an answer, a silent interval, another question, another interval, and I found myself gushing to fill the silence.

'Of course,' I remember saying, 'we'll pay for all the improvements necessary, and we won't ask you for anything.'

A long interval this time.

'I'll think about it,' said Harry Laity at last.

Outside as we walked back along the long, long lane, Jeannie exclaimed: 'You see, you didn't have to depend upon me. He was only interested in you. And you were very good, and I am sure you convinced him that we are genuine.'

We were to become close friends of Harry Laity; and there came a day when he confessed as to why he finally decided to rent us Minack.

'You remember when you said you would renovate the cottage at your own expense?'

'Yes,' I replied.

'Well,' he said, 'I looked at this very, very pretty girl beside you and said to myself: "She won't stick it for six months before deciding to go back to her glamorous London life . . . and then I'll have a renovated cottage which has cost me nothing."'

We were in the Old Success pub at Sennen Cove at the time, Jeannie beside me.

'There you are,' I said, turning to her, 'didn't I tell you as we walked down that long, long lane, that all you had to do was to be feminine, and Minack would be ours?'

Jeannie wrote *Meet Me at the Savoy* during our first two years at Minack. Danny Kaye wrote the Foreword. He had become a close friend of Jeannie during the time he made his first sensational appearance at the London Palladium. Jeannie gave him the manuscript to read and he loved it; and when, later, a magazine serialised the book, Jeannie went to meet him in London where a funny photograph was taken of them both at the Savoy. A photograph of Danny holding a pair of scissors and pretending to cut Jeannie's long dark hair.

We had decided on the title of the book before we left London. We used to churn over all sorts of alternatives as we sat in the lovely sitting room of our house at Mortlake, overlooking the finishing post of the Boat Race. It was a long room at the top of the house, oak beams and small windows, and a cavity where there was a fireplace; and above the fireplace was the ship's clock I bought for Jeannie at our first Christmas there, which today hangs in the galley kitchen of Minack. A bomb blasted the house soon afterwards, and though the sitting room became a shambles, the clock kept ticking.

One evening, when I had been striding up and down the room, I called out: 'I've got it!' We had been looking for a colloquial title, some phrase which could be in everyday use.

'What about *Meet Me at the Savoy*?'

'That's it!' said Jeannie.

I adopted the role of a bossy taskmaster while she wrote it.

I was well aware, like most of us, that Jeannie was only too ready to be sidetracked from her task; and so when she went into the chicken house where she was writing the book, I took the precaution of locking her in.

Sometimes I would hear a cry.

'Let me out! Let me out!'

Ruthlessly I would reply that she had only been at work for an hour.

'Let me out!'

And I would then comply.

The book, at last completed, had now to be sold to a publisher. We had confidently believed that there would be no difficulty in doing this. It was a surprising experience, therefore, when one solemn publisher after another said that the book was unsuitable. After all the years the book has proved to be a classic, and yet at the time no one wanted to know; Jeannie and I were without a friend when we most needed one. At last a small publisher accepted it, and gave an advance of £50. Jeannie, resilient Jeannie, was so delighted that she said she would buy something special for Minack with the money. The special something proved to be a number of Ganwick Cloches. Ganwicks were the vogue at the time; and by buying them both Jeannie and I believed that, thanks to *Meet Me at the Savoy*, we had started upon horticultural prosperity.

Shortly before the book was published, Jeannie was asked to write an article which had some connection with it. She chose to write an article called 'I Married an Author'. It is an article which mirrors her humour, her effervescence, and her warmth; and so I am recalling it:

I was always determined to marry an author. Like one of Ronald Searle's schoolgirls, I would puff my way along the promenade on our pre-breakfast run and discuss with my panting companions the topic of the day: Who would you like to marry if you could choose?

Opinion was evenly divided between the Master of the Hunt, a local millionaire, and a good-looking new curate. I was the only one who remained resolute in my choice . . . I wanted to marry an Author and he had to smoke a pipe.

Well I did marry an Author . . . and his pipe. And a few weeks after the wedding I was told of an elderly neighbour who, having borrowed my husband's book from the library, exclaimed in a shocked whisper, 'Oh I *do* hope Mrs Tangye hasn't read this!'

The book, *Time was Mine*, was the means of our meeting. I was the newly appointed Publicity Manager of the Savoy Hotel, and as such was expected to make suggestions for new books likely to interest the clients. Authors, therefore, were interested in meeting me and here was this author who, in a breathless rush, told me about his new book and asked me to put it on the bookstall. I did so. I also cajoled the Savoy barman to invent a new cocktail in its honour.

Yes, I married an Author . . . and his pipe.

But was I wise about the pipe? As I remove a glowing pipe that has been tucked forgetfully between two newly-laundered cushions, I ponder the wisdom of my schoolgirl's dream. True, the tobacco has a comfortable smell, and calmness reigns when the pipe is drawing well, but what about the ashes which smudge the clean tablecloth, and the daily cries of

'Where's my pipe? Have you seen my pipe?'

I have been wedded nine years to the Author and his pipe ... but I think I could do without the pipe.

The Author dislikes writing and when in a mood of creation must be treated very warily.

If I call out: 'Dinner is ready!' I am pretty certain to have hit the moment when the words have begun to flow.

Or thoughtlessly I may read out an item from a newspaper just when a sentence is being disentangled in his mind. I am more careful now but when I was a bride ...

At that time the Author had produced a book called *Went the Day Well?*, a collection of stories about men and women who had been killed in the early part of the war when Britain stood alone.

It was a very moving book and I felt a reflected pleasure when my boss, Mr Miles Thornewill, vice chairman of the Savoy Group, said of the introduction and epilogue: 'This is a most beautiful piece of prose.'

But the Author, whom I found curiously detached from other people's comment on his work, was already gathering material for his next book, a tome on the British Empire which was to run to 180,000 words and which he called *One King*.

Parcels of reference books arrived by every post; the sitting room was a mosaic of coloured maps; copies of past editions of Colonial reports, government and anti-government leaflets littered the chairs.

And the Author would go on working long after I had gone to bed, surrounded by the past and present of the British Empire.

When at last *One King* was published we were

on holiday in Cornwall and the first we heard of the stir it was going to make was when we had a telegram from a political friend: 'Emmanuel Shinwell is going round the House saying it is the most important book he has ever read.'

A few days later we were on the night train to London and arrived at Paddington on a cold November morning. Before we got into the taxi, we bought the Sunday papers. There on the book page of the *Sunday Times* a leading politician had begun his review with the words: 'This is a remarkable book . . .'

During the next few weeks the praise came from all quarters. Emmanuel Shinwell wrote in the *Evening News:* 'I would like to see every MP with a copy of this book.' The *Manchester Guardian* said: 'One could entrust the book to a foreigner seeking light on Imperial affairs.'

Some while later we met an aide of Field Marshal Montgomery.

'Your name Derek Tangye?' he asked, laughing. 'How we have cursed you at HQ. Monty made us all read *One King* and then cross-examined us as if we were at school!'

We both basked in the warm sun of praise and remembered with shivers some of the hurdles which had been overcome . . . not the least of which was when the chapter on India was lost in the post and the Author, unbelievably, had not taken a carbon copy, and had to write the whole complicated saga again.

Yes, I married an Author . . . there were many others I was to come to know. Some of them damaged a little the focus of my rose-tinted spectacles towards authors.

There was the bachelor who knew all about

gardens and women's hats and was full of merry humour. He had been the idol of my teenage, and when he wrote asking me, in my capacity of the Savoy Publicity Manager, to book a table in the Savoy Restaurant for a small dinner party, I went to endless trouble arranging everything in the most perfect detail.

The table reserved for celebrities was booked, I ordered an epicure's dinner; I told the head florist to garland the table with flowers and send the bill to me; and as it was a celebration party, I ordered a gala cake to be served and the bill for it also to be sent to me.

Then I sat back, and waited for the applause. But alas for the idol of my girlhood: I received a letter which ended, 'You may think it a very good stunt to put flowers and a cake on my table in order to step up the bill – and I imagine the hotel pays you well for this – but I have no intention of paying.'

I controlled myself and sent a very polite letter in reply, pointing out that the items concerned were the gift of the management. But I never heard from my once-favourite author again.

Then there was the lady, famous for her cookery books. She descended upon me before the publication of her new book, primly arch in her flowered toque.

'I'm just giving a little lunch for my publisher, and a few influential people, dear, and I want the menu to consist entirely of dishes from my new book . . . so if you'll take me along to see your chef I'll explain to him what I want.'

That poor maltreated chef who was famed among the cuisines of Europe: he climbed the stairs to my office, the spaniel eyes pleading beneath his white hat. 'Miss Nicol (my maiden name) for you anything . . . but this lady . . . no more!'

But I have other memories of authors. The gentle courtesy of Howard Spring and his pleasure at finding that his room overlooked the Thames; the battered hat and galoshes of Ernie Pyle, the greatest of all American reporters, and of our lunch together on his last day in England and of his certainty that he would soon be killed; the cosy humour of Sir Alan Herbert, and the shyness of John Steinbeck.

I was sitting in my office one morning when Steinbeck put his head cautiously round the door. 'I'm sorry to bother you,' he said. 'My name is John Steinbeck and I just wanted to thank you for booking my room and taking such good care of me' – he paused – 'and I wondered if you would care to have a drink with me . . . that's if you don't mind.'

Now that I also am an author, I wonder how any book is ever written at all. The sighing hours spent in front of a blank sheet of paper. The sudden glow of exultation when a sentence rushes into one's mind like the flow of water from a thawing pipe . . . and then the almost immediate trickle when everything seems to have been turned off at the main.

The days when one's mind is full and stupid, and the evenings, as a result, are made irritable. The moment when the cry in one's mind is: 'Why go on?'

And the weeks that follow the last full stop when one waits anxiously for the post and the publisher's verdict. All this is enough to make an author – or an authoress – difficult to live with.

But is it enough to turn a schoolgirl's dream into an illusion?

No. Decidedly, no.

There is an epilogue to her story in the article about the bachelor author, her teenage idol, who had misunderstood the special arrangements she had made for his dinner party. The bachelor author was Beverley Nichols; and he was to become a very close friend. I have written in a previous Minack Chronicle how we met him, but I will repeat the story because it is easy to forget the action of someone who helps you to change your life.

He was sitting in the office of a magazine editor who was late returning from lunch; and he picked up a proof copy of *A Gull on the Roof*, the first of the Minack Chronicles, began reading it, liked it, and told the editor when he arrived that he intended to devote his page to the book. The page was full of enthusiasm. My publisher was delighted, and sent us a telegram of congratulations. A very different mood on our part to that when I received the letter from a literary agent to whom I had first sent the manuscript: 'I'm disappointed by two reports that I have received on your book.'

Jeannie, at first, was to have the same kind of disappointing letter about *Hotel Regina* from a literary agent and, for that matter, from a publisher. She had spent two years writing *Hotel Regina*, the first of what was to become her hotel trilogy, the two others being *Home is the Hotel* and *Bertioni's Hotel*, and we hopefully despatched copies of the manuscript to a well-known publishing friend, and to a literary agent whose authors were among the most famous in the world.

As Jeannie's fiercest critic, I *knew* that *Hotel Regina*, dealing with the first period in London of the Second World War, was a beautiful book. Yet the literary agent wrote saying it was unpublishable. So did the publisher.

These two letters so angered me that I was glad we hadn't a telephone on the premises, because I would have picked it up and shouted abuse.

Instead I went to the little hut in the wood which we had specially bought to enable her to disappear and write her novel without being interrupted, carrying a bottle of champagne and two glasses. Then I went back to the cottage and collected her.

The bottle of champagne stood on the floor of the hut, two glasses beside it – and propped against the champagne bottle was a sheet of quarto typewriting paper upon which I had scrawled a well-known Cornish phrase: 'Bugger them all!'

Hotel Regina was not a conventional hotel novel. It portrayed the inside working of a hotel, the dramas that revolve around those who work in a hotel, and above all it had the mood of authenticity and of the atmosphere in London at the beginning of the Second World War.

Sir Alan Herbert, the wit, parliamentarian, playwright and author (Vivian Ellis wrote the lovely music for his *Bless the Bride*), known by the world of his time as APH, did much to launch *Hotel Regina* to success by a speech he made at the Savoy Hotel Annual General Meeting. His tall figure, his beak nose, his dishevelled hair, were a Savoy institution; he was often dropping in for lunch or drinks; and after the first night of one of his shows he would have a party in the Grill.

He treated Room 205, Jeannie's office, as his headquarters; and he would sometimes write his weekly article for *Punch* there, also his light-hearted verses for a Sunday newspaper. He would show the result of his verse to Jeannie; and sometimes she was ruthless in her comments: 'Alan, you can do better than that. It's awful!'

And occasionally he would arrive with a terrible

hangover, and he would say to Jeannie: 'I'm going to see Mr Somerset. Come with me.' Mr Somerset was the manager of Heppell's the chemist in the Strand, three minutes from the Savoy. He was noted for his chemical cocktail which was intended to cure a hangover.

APH's speech at the General Meeting was in his usual contemporary, witty style; and then he included a passage about *Hotel Regina*, reminding the audience of Jeannie's legendary association with the Savoy Hotel Company, and urging them to go out of the Meeting and buy a copy. Then he added, almost in the tone of a headmaster lecturing his pupils. 'Yes, I say buy it . . . don't borrow a copy!' At the time he was the leader of the battle to gain payment for authors from Public Library borrowing, and he never lost an opportunity to boost his campaign.

For instance, he had a private gimmick about his own books. If someone brought a book for him to sign, he would happily oblige and then, beneath his signature, would write the letters NTL.

The recipient of the signed copy would look at these three letters, puzzled.

'What do these letters mean?' Alan would be asked. And he would reply in mock solemnity:

'Not to lend.'

He was not just referring to his Public Library campaign for the payment to authors for book borrowing. He also had much experience of admirers coming up to him, and telling him that they had lent one of their favourite books to a friend, and now they could not remember which friend it was; and so they had lost their favourite book for ever.

So on this occasion, the occasion of the Savoy Hotel General Meeting, he urged his audience of shareholders to go out and buy *Hotel Regina*. This they apparently did because the book was soon out of print. The distinguished publisher and the literary agent with world-famous names as clients, had been proved wrong.

Jeannie, I feel, has never received proper recognition for her hotel trilogy. A reviewer on the BBC expressed the opinion that it was far more enjoyable than the notorious *Grand Hotel* by Vicki Baum; and others, like Mary Stewart, were entranced by it. Yet Jeannie, always doubtful about the value of her achievements, failed to exploit herself.

But there came a day when she changed her attitude. She felt so strongly about *Bertioni's Hotel*, the last of the trilogy, that she owed it to herself to come out of her shell. She decided she would go to London well before publication in order to plan promotion for the book; and also to prove her willingness to co-operate with those concerned in marketing it.

In due course we arrived in London, staying at Claridge's. Jeannie had a special fondness for Claridge's. It came, of course within her domain when she was Publicity Officer for the Savoy Group. One day she heard that a then unknown in Britain dress designer called Dior was staying there. Her instinct alerted her; and from the moment she used all her influence to help him. It was here that the delightful restaurant manager Milandra used to chase her around the tables when she arrived, well before luncheon time, to find out what distinguished people had booked tables for lunch. It was here that, a few days prior to the wedding of the Queen and Prince Philip, the best man, the Marquess of Milford Haven, knelt on the entrance steps of Claridge's in front of Jeannie, begging forgiveness for being late for their date. It was here that Jeannie introduced Baron, the famous photographer of his period, at his special request, to Fleur Cowles and her husband Mike, then owner of *Look* magazine. Baron had had a heavy lunch. A few days later he was with Jeannie in the Savoy Bar.

'Who's that man who has just come in?' asked Baron.

'Mike Cowles,' replied Jeannie.

'Do me a favour,' Baron quickly replied. 'I've always wanted to meet him.'

'You did!' laughed Jeannie.

A friend once said of Jeannie and me that we expected too much of people; and by that he did not mean to be critical. He just meant to convey his view that we were both too optimistic regarding people's attitudes and behaviour.

For instance, on this occasion, when Jeannie had decided to uproot herself from Minack in order to meet those who could help promote her book, she had a naive belief that by asking them to Claridge's and having a comfortable, easy drinking time in our suite, her personality would quietly create a euphoria, which would help exploit the book. We proceeded to welcome the newly appointed executive responsible for the possible exploitation; and for an hour we listened to stories of his family life. Jeannie never discussed her own book.

'I've no personality,' said Jeannie, laughing, after the person had left. 'If I had put on an act, pretended perhaps to be the reincarnation of Boudicca or someone,' she added, 'or had been cured of drugs, or been a reformed prostitute willing to tell her story, then I might have appeared interesting.'

Jeannie has an uncle (she had always called him uncle though he is really a cousin) called Canon Martin Andrews. He has recently had a party to celebrate his 100th birthday at which many of those who knew him during his many years as Rector of Stoke Climsland, near Callington, attended. At the party I heard him say to one ex-parishioner: 'I christened you, married, you, and who knows I'll bury you!' He lives alone in a lovely house overlooking the sea near Plymouth; and, understandably, because of his age, there are friends who are anxious about him.

'Don't want anyone around me, dearie,' he said to me. 'I like being on my own. You can behave foolishly without anyone knowing.'

He was a close friend of the Duke of Windsor. The Duke and Mrs Simpson used to visit him, discuss their problems, and there came a time when they asked him to marry them. But he felt he could not comply. He never gives any details of their intimate conversations. In his book, *Canon's Folly*, he skirts over them.

Jeannie and I have always called him Martin because he makes you feel that you belong to the same generation. There would be no age gap between anyone if people were not so conscious about age. 'I am an OAP,' says a letter to me, as if it is a badge of honour to carry.

Jeannie's habit was to telephone him regularly, calling from a public telephone box. Martin's voice is very loud, very clear.

'Dearie,' the trumpeting voice would come over the line, 'next time you ring, make it reverse charges!'

His passion, smoked salmon, was consigned to him from time to time by Jeannie.

'Oh my dear Jeannie,' I've heard him often say, 'you look after me so well.'

There was this great concourse of love for Martin from all areas of life. The Queen Mother had lunch with him once and cabbage was on the menu: 'Oh, how nice to see a plain English cabbage. Nobody ever gives us that!' He always receives a personal telegram from her on his birthday.

One evening, and this is the point of my digression, the Earl and Countess of Mount Edgcumbe invited

83

Jeannie and me to a party at their majestic home near Plymouth. Normally Jeannie and I would not have dreamed of going to such a party but there was a special endearing charm about the Edgcumbes which made us accept the invitation.

We had met them several times at luncheons given by Kim Foster, then chairman of the Cornwall County Council. They were comparatively recent arrivals in Cornwall, coming from New Zealand, where they had a sheep farm, after their cousin Mount Edgcumbe had died.

Jeannie, following our first meeting with them, made a shrewd comment: 'Effie loves their new situation, Edge hates it!'

Effie had a sweet nature, warm and giving, and it was easy to understand why she enjoyed the change from being a rancher's wife to that of being chatelaine of one of the great houses of Britain.

Edge, however, missed his sheep.

'Have you any sheep?' was one of the first questions he ever asked me. And I retaliated forever afterwards when we were together with the remark: 'If you give up Mount Edgcumbe and become a shepherd, that will be the day when we'll keep sheep.'

There were very many people at the party Jeannie and I attended; and, as always, Jeannie was soon wafted away to a part of the room where I would catch a sight of her surrounded by animated admirers. At parties we never remained side by side. We always were separate, never appearing to be man and wife.

Martin Andrews and I were left together. People gushed their stories to each other, but nobody gushed a story to us. We were standing by a pillar, and Martin Andrews turned to me and said: 'Nobody takes any notice of us at all. Have we *no* personality!?'

I told him then of Jeannie's effort to publicise *Ber-*

tioni's Hotel, and how her personality had no effect upon the person she was wanting to impress. And I added a story of my own which occurred in Hollywood when I was travelling round the world.

I was invited to lunch by a well-known Hollywood producer, and the other guest was Ray Milland. Neither of them seemed to notice me as we had pre-lunch drinks. Nobody seemed to notice my presence during the first course, the second course, and third course. I sat there mute, my ego building up a rage. And at last, in a desperate effort to gain attention, I burst.

'I think you both ought to know,' I said in a loud voice, 'that I am a fugitive from the police. I escaped from England because of the crime I had committed which will mean I could hang.' Then I paused, and announced dramatically: 'You see, I murdered my mother!'

My confession had no effect whatsoever. The producer and Ray Milland went on talking. I did not exist.

Jeannie rarely had such a fate. The dazzle about her attracted people quite apart from her delicious looks. Once, when we came to London from Minack, we were invited down to Pinewood Studios where Charlie Chaplin was directing Sophia Loren and Marlon Brando in the film he had written, the music for which he had composed, called *The Countess from Hong Kong*. We went into the studio where a scene was being 'shot', and stood quietly at the back.

Suddenly Charlie Chaplin stopped 'shooting' the scene. Apparently he had caught sight of Jeannie, and he came hurrying across the studio floor to where we were standing, and began to talk to her as if they had known each other all their lives. They had never pre-viously met. But he seemed to have instinctively realised that there was a special glow about her. A week later she was offered a contract to be the Publicity Officer for *The Countess from Hong Kong*. A wonderful compliment for which she was grateful, but she had no hesitation in refusing. She was happy in the life she had chosen.

Yet these stories about Jeannie, the contrast between those who intuitively sensed her qualities and those who failed to do so, provide an example of her character. Her qualities were there to see, to be appreciated, but she was not going to shout about them.

I have told how Beverley Nichols helped *A Gull on the Roof* when it was first published. His brother Paul was the Vicar of Sancreed near Penzance, the church where Stanhope Forbes is buried; and we heard one day, soon after his article had been published, that he was staying there. Jeannie, as it was peak daffodil harvest time, rushed out and picked armfuls of Magnificence, the first early yellows. Then we hurried over to Sancreed, only to find he had just left.

It was quite a long while after that before we first met, and our friendship began. This first meeting involved asking him and his brother to lunch. We anxiously awaited their arrival, peering out of the window to see whether a car was coming down the winding lane; and when at last we saw the car, we found to our surprise that it had stopped at Monty's Leap. I hurried down to meet it; and out of the car stepped Beverley.

'I hope you don't mind,' he said, and to my surprise he appeared nervous, then with a smile, 'I want to pay my respects to Monty.'

Monty the cat who, sharing our adventure, had come with us from London; and of whom I had written in *A Cat in the Window*. He was buried by the little stream called Monty's Leap where the car had stopped.

Homage having been paid, he said to me: 'Any

dramas?' And in a tone that he was hoping for one. Then added in a conspiratorial fashion: 'Paul and I are not quite seeing eye to eye at the moment!' It was said mischievously. No bite in it.

Over the years he was to come again and again to Minack. And we have sat listening to him tell stories, gossiping stories of the people he had known, hour after hour.

'I was staying with Willie Maugham at Cap Ferrat, and one of the other guests was a high ranking Foreign Office official. As we were standing on the steps saying goodbye to him, a servant passed with his luggage, and one of the suitcases burst open. To everyone's horror, four first editions of Willie's books fell on the floor. The Foreign Office official had pinched them!'

Then there was the story of Syrie Maugham, estranged wife of Somerset Maugham, who always remained in love with him. She was dying, and knew it, and she was lying in bed in her suite at the Dorchester where Beverley was visiting her. While he was there she summoned the hotel hairdresser, pulling as she did so, a lace shawl around her shoulders. There she was, pillows as a backrest, when she said to Beverley: 'I want to look nice . . . just in case Willie might come.'

He didn't.

One day, and I cannot remember which year, Beverley was sitting after lunch in the corner of the sofa, quietly watching Jeannie as she fussed over the washing up in the galley of a kitchen.

'Jeannie,' he said, 'you had the whole world open for you, a great career waiting for you. There was not a country where you did not have friends to give you a márvellous time. You were loved. People felt so much better just being with you. Why did you turn your back on that world?'

She stopped fussing over the washing up, and came out of the galley of a kitchen. She was wearing an apron, the large head of a donkey printed upon it, which somebody had given her.

'Darling Beverley,' she replied, and there was a teasing note in her voice, 'you know enough about the fickleness of that kind of life . . .'

'Yes, I agree.'

Then Jeannie went on.

'I was lucky enough to find out early that there is no happiness to it except in fits and starts. And I was lucky enough to have Derek who felt the same.

'We both wanted to create our own roots, be independent of employers, never have our future at risk by take-overs.

'And we had to start creating these roots *in time*.'

SEVEN

The daffodil season was over, and we were free, and the March morning was soft and warm, and the air had the miracle mixture of sea scents, and daffodil scents, and primrose scents, and growing scents of juvenile plants and grasses. I went out in my dressing gown to give chocolate biscuits to Merlin who was leaning over the fence by the stables; and when I returned I said to Jeannie, 'Let's have breakfast down the cliff beside the sea.' And she had agreed; 'Give me ten minutes,' adding, 'I've got tongue and I'll cut bread and butter, and I'll put the percolator on for the coffee.' We were snobs about coffee. We had the roasted beans sent to us from London by Whittards of Fulham Road, most distinguished of tea and coffee merchants, founded towards the end of the last century. Then we put the beans into our electric grinder, and, whether it was true or not, we always believed our coffee was better than any other.

We were ready to go: tongue and bread and butter wrapped in foil had been placed in a basket, so too the thermos of coffee, so too a couple of cups and knives – when there were cat problems.

A rattlesnake sound from Ambrose.

'Ambrose wants something,' I called out. Jeannie was in the spare bedroom.

'Give him something out of the tin,' she called back.

'But there isn't anything in the tin,' I replied.

'There are spare ones on the second shelf in the kitchen.'

I found one. Beef with Kidney, the label said; and I picked up a tin opener, cut round the lid, and was met by a repulsive odour. Ambrose did not mind the odour. As soon as my scooped portion was on the small plate in front of him, he was ravenously eating it.

'All's well,' I called out. 'Ambrose is satisfied.'

A moment's silence. Then Jeannie's voice from the spare room.

'Did you give him any milk? He'll want fresh milk.'

I love cats, but I so understand my other self which hated them, and which writhed at the way cat lovers fussed over them. My other self thought they were mindless and cruel and selfish and, because they would not come running to you, as a dog will come in natural friendliness, that they were incapable of affection.

Yet, with Jeannie as my instructress, I was to learn how wrong I had been. Cats, I was to learn for instance, respond to subtlety, and they have a strong measure of extrasensory powers which enables them to anticipate situations to their advantage. Unimaginative people, insensitive people, or people like my other self who was brought up in the belief that cats were vermin, will not of course agree with me. Indeed the customary attitude of such people is to treat cats as a joke, a sick joke at that. One of the most successful cat books ever written described the 101 ways to use a dead cat.

However, as a convert, I saw the light; and with Jeannie's guidance over the years I began to appreciate those remarks about cats, and the behaviour of cats themselves, which I would have dismissed as sentimental nonsense in my other-self days.

The definition, for instance, by Beverley Nichols of a subtle person. A subtle person is F (Feline). An insensitive person is non-F. Then there is the immortal phrase of Paul Gallico who, when describing a cat placed in a dilemma, wrote: 'When in doubt wash.'

I was to learn, for instance, that cats are great time-wasters. You will be sitting in an armchair and about to get up when the cat of the household decides to jump upon your lap and, as a result, you remain immobile; and, in order to justify your immobility, you try to twist and turn without disturbing the cat in order to reach pen and paper for note-making – failing, because pen and paper are *just* out of reach.

I was to learn, also, the art of stroking: the need to stroke a cat delicately, tracing a gentle finger down the back, a gentle finger criss-crossing the forehead, a gentle finger tickling under the ears, that as a result a cat's conventional purr erupts into a purr of falsetto proportions.

I was also to learn how cats sabotage good intentions when, lying in bed in the morning, feeling guilty that you are not up and about, and at last saying to yourself: 'Action stations! I'm going to get up!' the cat, in my case Ambrose, jumps on the bed because he has decided that lying on my chest, fur close to my nostrils, suits his mood of the moment. What do I do? I never believed it possible when I hated cats that I would lie in bed with one on my chest, obediently letting him stay there.

I have learnt, too, that when one is lying, or sitting, believing one is doing the cat a favour by enduring the discomfort, the cat is believing he is doing *you* a favour. It is not me who, in order to be free, dislodges Ambrose, but Ambrose who dislodges himself. He has had enough of me. He has made his gesture. He has he believes, humoured me; and so he can leave me, jumping off the bed, jumping off the chair.

I often wonder how those who have three cats, four

cats, five cats, dispense in fair proportions their affection for each cat. I, as it happens, cannot cope with multiple love. I am one-track-minded. I admire those who embrace with their love all children, all cats, all donkeys, all anything, but I am unable to share such an embracing love. I love individually, just like Jeannie has done. It is as if we open a door by an inch or two, see the chink of light and concentrate upon it. Open the door wider, wider and wider, and concentration becomes blurred by the expanse which is on view. One sees, as a consequence, a landscape instead of a portrait.

We do not today live in a real world. We live, for the most part, as observers watching pictorial experiences of television crews; and listening to commentators, brilliant in their fluency. Next morning when we see a friend we say: 'What did you think of last night's programme . . .' Or: 'I'm so cross I didn't switch the video on, and so I missed that programme on Channel Four!'

This second-hand living is far, far away, for instance, from Laurie Lee's *Cider with Rosie*, that love story of youth. Rosie, if the setting was today, would not have had the time for her languid teasing. She would have had an appointment with a soap opera.

I have, therefore, learnt to appreciate that Ambrose who has performed an imaginary favour by lying upon my chest when I have decided to get up in the morning, or has pinioned me in my chair, or who has exasperated me by miaowing at me to open another tin, is a reflection of everyday reality. I am not watching on a screen. I am living reality.

There is another aspect to this reality. I did not believe Jeannie is those early days when she said that cats had a natural desire to give love; and I laughed at her. Cats give love? These vermin which were cruel and

92

selfish? My future mother-in-law, after hearing one of my outbursts on the subject, remarked to her daughter: 'I don't think, dear, that such an anti-cat man will be suitable as a husband for you.'

But I have learnt as the Monty years, the Lama years, the Oliver years, the Ambrose and Cherry years have gone by, that a cat can give you such true love that you begin to worry what would happen if you were run over by a bus. For I have learnt since my anti-cat time that a cat can love a person, exclusively, although the person has to earn that love by developing an uncanny sense of union with the cat concerned. Sad to think there will be those who read this who will say I am writing sentimental rubbish. Yet love, from whatever direction it may come, is the only true generator of happiness. So why throw scorn on it, whether it comes from a cat, a budgerigar, a dog, a hamster, a guinea pig, a donkey? The pursuit of materialism may provide us with the delights of high tech, but it can never provide us with that sudden glow which is love.

Ambrose has his milk in a small bowl and, as a result of Jeannie's query, I filled it, warming the milk with a drop of hot water from the kettle. Jeannie appeared as I bent down to put the bowl beside Ambrose.

'Come on,' I said, 'now we can go.'

We shut the front door, having left the bedroom window open for Ambrose to go out if he so wished; and then we sauntered down the path, Annie's Folly on our right (the *Macrocarpa* which we had acquired as a three-foot high Mediterranean heather but was now a thirty-foot high tree), the newly acquired water butt on the corner of the cottage on our left; and then down we walked towards the gate which opens on the path that leads to the sea.

'Oh Jeannie,' I said, groaning, 'just look who is following us!'

It was Cherry.

'Now what do we do?'

We wanted a peaceful breakfast beside the sea, but first there was Ambrose to hold us back, now there was Cherry; and I had noticed also on the other side of the gate which we had to open on the way down to the cliff, a menacing Merlin.

'Jeannie,' I said, 'we're never free. We pretend we are free. We tell people how wonderful it is to live in a beautiful place where the only traffic is the distant hum of a fishing vessel, where there are no neighbours to observe us, where there is no telephone to interrupt us – and yet we are not free at all. We are dominated by these two cats and a donkey.'

'And the gulls on the roof,' Jeannie added.

'Yes, the gulls on the roof,' I said.

The gulls, four regulars, screamed out for their breakfast, screamed out for their lunch, screamed out for their supper; and there was also the evening gull. This gull came as dusk was falling, flighting up from the rocks, settling on the apex of the roof, then waiting for me to observe it. And I would then throw something up in the gloaming, and he would clutch it in his beak, and fly silently away towards the rocks and the

Jeannie, photographed by Baron (*Baron*)

At the Savoy Hotel after a theatre first night

Arriving at the old Berkeley
Hotel in Berkeley Street,
Mayfair

Leaving Richmond Church

The bathroom was unconnected to the cottage when this photograph was taken (*Malindine*)

Feeding Queen Mary and the other chickens

Jeannie with Lama, Penny and Fred

The day the QE2 visited Minack. Her siren sounded and
Penny and Fred hooted in reply

A donkey picnic with Penny and Fred (*Michael Murray/Woman's Weekly*)

Cherry

Jeannie on the tractor (*Michael Murray/Woman's Weekly*)

Our last photograph together, outside the cottage (*David Wills*)

sea. And sometimes I would forget to feed it. I would be digressed into doing some other task like fetching the coal, and night would fall, and I would suddenly remember.

'Oh Jeannie,' I would say, 'I forgot to feed the evening gull!'

But here was Cherry at our heels, wanting to come with us on our breakfast walk, and I had no intention of allowing her to do so. I wanted a *quiet* breakfast, a languid breakfast with Jeannie beside me watching the foam creaming the rocks, idly talking about events and thoughts. Cherry would bring anxiety. Cherry would first have to face Merlin in the path, and Merlin, sometimes, liked to pretend he was a hound chasing a fox when he saw either Ambrose or Cherry. Then on the walk down the narrow, twisting path to the rocks, there were a couple of badger sets; and Cherry, out of cat curiosity, was in danger of going down one of them. I just could not cope with Cherry as a breakfast companion. So what to do?

The answer, of course, was an easy, though inconvenient one. I had to traipse back to the cottage, and scoop more out of the tin with the repulsive odour on to a saucer, place the saucer down in front of Cherry who had followed me – and then run.

Only Merlin was now an obstacle between us and our breakfast. Jeannie, however, had solved this problem. She had remembered the five pounds of carrots we had bought the previous day, and that they were still in the car; and while I was dealing with Cherry, she had collected three or four. Merlin was delighted. Munch, munch, munch . . . and we scurried away from him down the path, quickly opened the white gate, then on down the twisting path, a path which does not look like a path for humans . . . indeed, except by ourselves, it is only used by the badgers.

We came to the top of the cliff, and to the steps, earth-made steps, which led to the first of our small, sloping meadows, and to a particular one called by us the Jack Train meadow.

Jack Train was a radio star in his time, a pivot of the famous Tommy Handley programme. A gimmick he had was to pretend he was always seeking an alcoholic drink, and he had a famous catch phrase in reply to anyone who asked him on the programme whether he would like to have a drink.

'I don't mind if I do,' was his reply.

This catch phrase had inevitable results.

Whenever Jack was at a function or just enjoying himself by a visit to a pub, there were always a number of people who would offer him a drink, just to hear him say: 'I don't mind if I do.'

Jeannie and I had known him for a long time and, as it happens, he was a very moderate drinker.

'But,' as he put it once to us, 'how can I disappoint my public?' Nevertheless he *did* disappoint his public. Often he would accept the offered drink, then pass it to someone else. He was a lovable, gentle person.

One early summer he was engaged to help promote a television company, and the promotion included a train travelling around the West Country exhibiting the advantages of this company. Jack Train was the star the company needed to attract the public.

About this time Jeannie and I had been invited to lunch by a distinguished local dignitary. Our attendance at the lunch began badly. We had been instructed in a letter by the dignitary to arrive at a certain time, and that a car would be waiting to take us on the final stage of the journey to his home. Unfortunately the wife of this dignitary did not know of this letter; and we were greeted by the car driver with the words: 'I suppose you realise you are a quarter of an hour late!'

Good manners restrained Jeannie and me from disclosing the contents of the letter of instructions; and we proceeded to the home, and soon were engaged in that unreal chatter which takes place when one is launched into a room where everyone is a stranger. Then we went into lunch, and I saw that Jeannie had been placed at the right of the host. I chattered to my neighbours, either side of me. Everybody chatted, though in low tones. It was that kind of party.

Suddenly, however, halfway through the lunch, and I had on the plate in front of me roast lamb, fresh green peas and Cornish new potatoes, there was a mild commotion at the end of the table where Jeannie was sitting beside the host. I stopped listening to my neighbours, instead listened to the voice of an enraged Jeannie. Jack Train was being attacked! And, as I learnt later from Jeannie, he was being accused of being a chronic drunk, and that it was crazy of the television company to have employed him.

For a brief moment this conventional lunch party was lit up by passion. Jeannie was being loyal to a friend, and she did not care how conventional-minded people might think of her. Then normal conversation was resumed, so too my consuming of roast lamb, fresh green peas and Cornish new potatoes.

This morning, as I wrote these words, the postman brought me a letter from Jeannie's Auntie Mirrie, now over ninety, and Jeannie's godmother. I had asked her what she remembered most about Jeannie . . . and she had replied in her letter: 'Loyalty . . . always loyal to her true friends. Even as a child she was always kind, not only to people, to all living things.'

Auntie Mirrie went on: 'She was given a kitten when the family lived at Sopwell Lodge, St Albans. It became ill I think with distemper. Her mother had its basket removed to the garage. It got worse and the vet said it would no doubt have to be put to sleep. Jeannie burst into tears and said, "Oh no, Oh no . . . let Auntie Mirrie have it. She will get it better!" And we took it to our own home, and soon it completely recovered.'

Then there was Auntie Mirrie's story of the Fairy Ring.

'We used to take Jean and Barbara for picnics in Welwyn Woods, and one day we were walking along chatting and laughing when Jeannie stopped dead, and whispered: "Hush! I see a Fairy Ring!"'

'We all gazed. There was a tree and just in front of it . . . a perfectly round circle of dark green grass. The other grass all around was the palest possible green. We were all astounded. I had never seen one before. Jeannie said that the fairies will be dancing on it tonight; and we crept very quietly away.'

Jeannie had told me this story. She told me it when, one summer's day years ago near a cove called Penberth, we were exploring the crevices, long disused tiny meadows, gloriously aware of the fun of life, scrambling up rocks, resting on one jutting out to sea, saying in our minds that we were in love, and we were on holiday, and one day we would live on this Cornish coast for ever, thinking of mad hopes because we were free, because we were far, far away from sensible decisions, because we were intoxicated by the sense of antiquity which makes the passing fashions of mankind a laughing stock – there we were together when, suddenly, Jeannie said: 'Hush . . . look, over there beneath that rock, is a Fairy Ring!'

Not a ring of dark green grass this time. A ring of daisies. 'The fairies will be dancing there tonight,' said Jeannie, just as she had said when she was a child.

The daffodils in the Jack Train meadow were old-fashioned ones called Irving. They were yellow trumpets, and lovely to look at, outside or indoors, but progress had decreed that they were no longer suitable for the public. The public required, according to the merchants, more sophisticated varieties; and so, luckily for them, the Irvings of Jack Train's meadow are never picked. I remember him standing there in the afternoon before the lunch party I have described.

'Go on,' I said, 'pick some, and take them back to London.'

A pause. Then:

'I don't mind if I do.'

We had names for other meadows also. There was, for instance, Shelagh's meadow which is on a steep slope, and has Magnificence daffodils growing there, another yellow trumpet but more up to date than Irvings. Shelagh had a special love for this meadow and I don't know why. She just seemed to have an affinity with it, as if she had been there before, and it had become a friend. Shelagh was the illegitimate pretty waif whom I wrote about in *A Drake at the Door*, who died bicycling to work at Minack. Tender, shy Shelagh who had just celebrated her twenty-first birthday.

She used to leave her bicycle in the stables; and that morning when she died, at the exact moment as I learnt later that she died, I heard the wheels of her bike rasping the grey chippings as she turned the corner beneath our bedroom window.

'Shelagh has arrived,' I said to Jeannie.

We had names for other meadows. We had one, for instance, called *The Times* meadow. *The Times*, for a reason I cannot remember, sent a photographer with two assistants to take photographs of our daffodil meadows. I remember dithering around posing this way and that with Jeannie, often bent double as we picked, and in so doing not looking our best; and sometimes standing upright, the sea behind us, holding bunches of daffodils in our arms.

None of them, however, was the photograph which *The Times* picture editor favoured. He chose one instead which I cherish. It is a photograph of Jeannie with the two girls, Shelagh, and Jane (also of *A Drake At the Door*), standing together beside a sloping meadow of Obvallaris, the miniature King Alfred: it is so simple.

There were other signposts of our lives as we went down the foot-wide path to the rocks. There was, for instance, the crevice beneath a great boulder of a rock where we believe Lama was born – believing it because years later, Daisy, a little grey wild cat which we were sure was the mother of Lama, was found by us to be nursing another little black kitten in the crevice beneath the great boulder of a rock. The strange story as to how we link Oliver to this little kitten is too complicated to explain here. It is a magical, yet true story, and I have told it in *A Cat Affair*.

The meadows we were walking past were potato meadows before we planted the daffodil bulbs. We had created these tiny-sized meadows ourselves, delving them out of the cliff slope, cutting the undergrowth away, watching Tommy Williams, a tall, gaunt Cornishman, doing the really hard work by digging the ground with his long-handled Cornish shovel.

I was to use such a shovel myself when the time for harvesting the potatoes arrived, the specially flavoured Cornish new potatoes of that period. They were delicacies, and treated by the cliff growers as such. The seed potatoes from which the harvest came had names like May Queen and the Duke of York, but you do not find such potatoes now. The market requires large tasteless potatoes which will be covered by manufactured sauces. No longer is there a market for the small, exquisitely flavoured Cornish new potato because it is uneconomical. It has no bulk.

But when Jeannie and I began at Minack, May Queen and the Duke of York were much in demand as the first of the earlies; and, like other cliff growers, we took immense pride in sending the best samples away to market. Each potato, for instance, had to be free from any speck of earth, and we would place them in a special basket called a chip, and each chip would hold 12lb. The bottom of the chip would be lined with white paper, and, when it was full, potato leaves would first cover them, then a cardboard sheet. We would weigh, string up and, load into the tractor the previous day's digging in the early morning of the following day, dawn breaking. We had an iron tripod, the weighing machine attached by a hook; and I would weigh while Jeannie tied up each chip with string.

There was such joy in those moments: here was the moment of personal achievement, the realisation of a reward that millionaires cannot buy. We had turned the ground in the autumn, we had bought the seeds, 'shot' them in a hut till their sprouts appeared, then planted them, watched them peep through the soil, then hoed them, been anxious about them, worrying whether storm or frost might destroy them ... and now it was all over. They were on their way to market.

Jeannie and I were besotted by potatoes at this period. Our livelihood, and our future, depended upon them. I kept a log book, and its contents reflect our tunnel-vision attitude towards potatoes. There is no mention of other events in our lives. No descriptions of sights around us. No record of those who visited us. Just an endless record of our infatuation with potatoes.

Here are a few entries:

19 January

Started to plant potatoes. Planted three trays of Dukes down the cliff, one tray of May Queen. We now have so many meadows down the cliff that I must number them, so keep check on their usefulness.

20 January

Planted almost two trays of Dukes in the very bottom cliff meadow. None of them well shooted. Sowed fertiliser in the furrows.

24 February

Potato planting at last finished with five baskets of Pilot, not overcut but very medium-shooted in last year's violet meadow. Ground heavy.

12 March

Tom Laity [our farmer neighbour] does not seem happy about the potato crop. Those showing above ground do not look strong. Another farmer said there were few stinging nettles growing yet. 'Few stinging nettles,' he says, 'mean a bad potato harvest.'

20 March

I met an old farmer today who used to grow potatoes at the next-door farm, and he said: 'Only expect a good harvest every four years ... they keep you in funds for the other three.'

19 April

Good news, there has been so much rain that

the big potato growers haven't planted any potatoes. That means we'll have the early market to ourselves. Jeannie and I are thrilled!

24 April

We went down to the pub at Lamorna this evening, and Tommy Bailey said they are all saying we've got the best-looking growing potatoes on the cliff. Jeannie and I felt so proud . . . but we are no nearer drawing [local word for harvesting].

10 May

So frustrating, cold weather and dry, and the potatoes are not moving.

16 May

Jeannie and I went down the cliff, and furrowed with our hands under a few plants, and came back with a nice amount of Dukes for ourselves.

24 May

At last we dug a chip, just a chip. And we sold it locally.

29 May

We are away! We went down the cliff before breakfast, and I started digging, and Jeannie picking up. Then Tommy arrived, and we really got going. We ended the day with thirty-six chips of Dukes and May Queen, and Tommy and I carried them up to the top, and left them in what they called the cemetery field because old cattle were buried there; and tomorrow, very early, Jeannie and I will start weighing them.

At all times it was Jeannie's enthusiasm, her never-doubting confidence in our life together at Minack that kept me, so often, from financial despair. Jeannie was carefree about money. Her sister Barbara tells how, if she was given a pound when she was a child, she would cherish it. Jeannie, when given a pound, would quickly spend it. On the other hand when she was broke, when we both were broke, she never moaned. She was perpetually propelled by an optimism that convinced her all would soon be well. There was a moment at Minack when we did not even have the money for a postage stamp, yet Jeannie was undaunted. There was never an occasion when she was tempted to say: 'We must go back to London where we can earn a decent living'; never an occasion when she doubted the wisdom of her decision to give up one of the most glamorous jobs in London. A columnist in the *Daily Mail* wrote at the time she left:

Jean is slim, colleen-like, with green eyes and dark hair who seems so young and innocent and delicately pretty that you couldn't imagine her saying 'Boo' to all sorts of important people including tough American correspondents.

For ten years she has been a key woman at that international rendezvous of film stars, politicians, maharajahs, financiers, business men and what have you . . . the Savoy Hotel.

She is about to quit the post of publicity boss or public relations officer for the Savoy, the Berkeley, and Claridge's. Her job consisted not only of keeping those hotels before the public eye but in stopping indiscreet stories from appearing in the newspapers and sometimes in protecting timid guests from the glare of publicity. Now that is a job requiring tact, intelligence, and charm, and Jean has all three qualities.

Who stopped the story about the colonel (with the DSO) who was working in the kitchens of the Savoy from getting into the papers? Jean Nicol Tangye. Who arranged Dior's first interview in this country? The same girl. When Ernie Pyle the famous war correspondent (they made a movie about him) was going off to his death in the Pacific he had his last lunch with Jean. He told her sadly: 'I'll never see you again. There's been too much luck in my life, and it's exhausted.'

Close friend of Danny Kaye, Tyrone Power, Gertrude Lawrence, Bob Hope, Bing Crosby . . . there isn't a famous name in the past decade that doesn't know Jean.

Well, she is going to retire for she thinks that ten years is enough in the glare of London's West End. And she is right.

It was very hot those first two months at Minack, and it was like a furnace down the cliff as we dug our early potatoes. We often worked together on our own and, because the ambiance of the beautiful scenery and its loneliness made us feel we were on a South Sea island, Jeannie would be naked as she picked up the potatoes while I, wearing boots, dug them up with my long-handled Cornish shovel.

Then after a while, Jeannie would suddenly say she had had enough and was going to have a bathe; and she would run away from me, down the foot-wide track to the rocks and the sea. I would watch her, this gazelle-like creature, and ponder how such a short while ago she was daily playing the role of a sophisti-cated hostess at the Savoy or the Berkeley or Claridge's.

She would pause at the point where the track fell steeply and took her out of the sight. She would pause, and wave at me, her long dark hair falling over her bare shoulders. A few seconds later, gulls disturbed from their somnolent ruminating, rose from the rocks calling their weird cries; and telling me that Jeannie had arrived at the rock pool where she bathed.

Now here we were again years later, about to have a picnic breakfast close to where we dug the potatoes, and nothing had really changed. The rocks stared at the sea, the sea churned at the rocks. A cormorant was drying its wings on the other side of our teaspoon of a bay. Primroses were in clumps. Blackthorn was coming into white bridal flower in inaccessible places along the cliff. We were, as in the beginning, blissfully happy, and Jeannie in her looks had been untouched by time. More than ever we were aware that if one is to have solid happiness, one has to have roots, then build on them. The roots will be there to comfort you in time of trouble.

We sat on a grass bank just above the rock where Lama sat when I took a photograph of her, the photograph that became the cover of my book *Lama*. Jeannie spread butter on a slice of bread, covered it with tongue and handed it to me; and as she did so a scene in the previous night's television news passed through my mind: a scene showing rows of madmen screaming into telephones, each with a miniature television screen in front of them. Screaming madmen of London, New York and Tokyo manipulating the world's money markets.

But for Jeannie and me we were sharing a halcyon moment of idleness that reached into our souls.

No intellectual turmoil disturbing us into feeling guilty because we were happy. We were alone, together.

We were alone with an untarnished private world around us that stretched back unchanged through the centuries, placing modern mankind's madness into perspective.

EIGHT

We did not return to the cottage until after mid-day.
We had letters to write. I had chapter five of *The
Cherry Tree* to begin. Jeannie had a painting to do.
There was the washing up, the rooms to tidy, someone
might call. But we didn't care.

It was a mid-March morning like a June morning. A
zephyr of a breeze, and the sun sparkling its golden
rays on the calm sea, warming our faces. There were
pools of currents on the sea, and they resembled light-
coloured lakes. To our right were the Bucks, two
clusters of rocks which look like a pugilist's fists. That
morning, at low tide, the waves were lapping so gently
against them that gulls had gathered upon them, silent.
We lay back on the grass, Jeannie saying it was damp,
but we didn't care.

'How lucky we are,' said Jeannie, using her favourite
phrase, 'that we can share this together.'

And as she spoke I thought of a passage from Emily
Brontë's diary. 'It's past twelve o'clock,' she wrote.
'Anne and I have not tidied ourselves, done our bed
work, or done our lessons, and we want to go out and
play.'

I have thought sometimes of Jeannie as a mirror of
Emily, as I have also thought of her sometimes as a
mirror of Scarlett O'Hara. Both very different it is
true, but Jeannie had this contrast in her character.

Emily the gentle side, Scarlett the passionate side. Emily the dreamer, Scarlett the doer with the passion for the land she loved, and the will to defend her Tara at any price. But on this morning Jeannie was Emily.

In *Shirley*, whose character she based on Emily, Charlotte Brontë wrote:

> In Shirley's nature there prevailed at times an easy indolence: there were periods when she took delight in perfect vacancy of hand and eye, moments when her thoughts, her simple existence, the fact of the world being around, and heaven above her, seemed to yield her such fulness of happiness that she did not need to lift a finger to increase the joy. Often, after an active morning, she would spend a sunny afternoon in lying stirless on the turf ... no spectacle did she ask but that of the deep blue sky, and such cloudlets that sailed afar and aloft across its span; no sound but that of a bee's hum, the leaf's whisper. Her sole book in such hours was the dim chronicle of memory, or the sibyl page of anticipation ... round her lips at moments played a smile which revealed glimpses of the tale or prophecy: it was not sad, not dark.

We lay there for a minute or two, silent, thinking irrationally; and my thoughts revolved around how the first Tangye who came to Cornwall was a Breton and the name was spelt Tanguy (the Tanguy name is well known in Brittany). My thoughts prompted me to think that, although I always proudly proclaim myself as Cornish, I am not in fact true Cornish: my Breton ancestors only came here in the thirteenth century. What prompted me in thinking this way was that on our left, high above on our left, was the standing rock called Carn Barges overlooking Mount's Bay. The first

Tanguy almost certainly sailed into Mount's Bay, landing at Mousehole or Penzance (the first parish record of a Tanguy was at Madron close to Penzance); and there to the left and above us was the standing rock of Carn Barges which he must have seen.

Jeannie's irrational thoughts were not of a serious nature, however. She began to laugh, as she lay beside me. 'I was thinking of the fisherman who smashed his rod, snapping it across his knees because the fish he thought he had caught had got away!'

We had watched the incident with astonishment. It was an August afternoon, and the fisherman was standing on the other side of our bay on a rock, casting his line, then slowly drawing it in. We watched him for a few minutes, and he seemed peaceful enough, and we were intrigued as to what he would catch. A pollock probably, possibly a mackerel, or perhaps a horrid-tasting boney wrass. We watched him winding in the line, and there was an air of hopeful expectancy about him.

Then suddenly all hell let loose. The fisherman started to shout, to curse, to use terrible language until finally we watched the climax of his fury, due presumably to the escape of his fishy victim.

Shouting his anger to the world, we watched him grab his rod and break it into pieces across an outstretched knee, as if he were breaking a branch for use on a domestic fire.

I remember wondering at the time what might have caused his behaviour. Those who suddenly erupt will be judged by the eruption itself. Yet, more often than not, a series of incidents, emotional disappointments, a let-down by a friend or an associate, a love affair gone wrong, provide the spark which ignites the eruption. A fish escaping from a line, therefore, can be the lightning conductor.

I reminded Jeannie of another holiday season incident. At the time there had been several stories of helicopters rescuing climbers in Wales and Scotland; and one afternoon I heard cries coming from the direction of the cliff. One often hears cries in the countryside. Farmers are calling their cows because it is milking time, a wife of a farmer is calling her husband because a visitor has called; and in our case there is an added problematical call – that of the skin diver who has surfaced from his undersea adventure and is calling his mother boat to collect him. At first I thought the cries I heard did, in fact, come from a skin diver.

But they persisted, and I went off down towards the cliff to find out what caused them. I soon found out. A young man had lost himself in the undergrowth and brambles between Carn Barges and Minack; and was shouting: 'I want a chopper! Send for a chopper to rescue me!'

Three gannets pounded their huge wings a mile offshore, flying westward; and a minute later we watched a bundle of dunlins flying at speed in the same direction, skimming the sea. Where, I wondered, were they going?

Another few moments of silence, then Jeannie said she was thinking of A. P. Herbert, and how, when he used to stay with us, he would make his way to the rock pools, and collect limpets for Hubert, our first gull on the roof.

Jeannie in *Meet Me at the Savoy* tells how she met Alan Herbert:

'Hullo,' said a man's voice. I was standing on the steps leading down to the Restaurant foyer.

'Hullo,' I said without looking round.

'I've been thinking,' said the voice, 'that it was high time we met.'

I turned in surprise. Facing me was a thin figure in the uniform of a Petty Officer. The features and remarkable nose were surmounted by wispy grey hair, giving him the appearance of an amiable pelican.

'And now that we've introduced ourselves,' he began.

'But we haven't,' I said firmly.

'Well, I know who you are . . . and I am Petty Officer Herbert at your service!'

'Oh,' I exclaimed delighted, 'you're A. P. Herbert, I should have known. How I loved *The Water Gypsies!* My grandmother used to read it every six months . . . it was her favourite book.'

'I could do with a little less of the grandmother,' replied APH, 'but I will overlook it this time, and buy you a small gin.'

And then years later, on a summer morning at Minack, he would collect his toy bucket which he had bought specially for the purpose, and walk off towards the cliff, and down the steep path to the rocks around the pool where we bathed when the tide was low. He would be away two or three hours while Jeannie and I pursued our customary tasks, and then he would return, toy bucket full of limpets, and he would open them, and call out to Hubert who was nowhere to be seen: 'Hubert! Hubert! Where are you?' And it was uncanny how often a few minutes later Hubert would appear, settle on the roof, and receive ravenously the limpets APH threw to him.

There was another aspect of Alan's association with Hubert. One evening the three of us were listening to a Promenade concert: the orchestra was being conducted by Sir Malcolm Sargent, and the symphony being played was César Franck's Symphony in D

Minor. At one stage of the symphony Hubert began a noisy gull scream on the roof; and Alan went out of the cottage, looked up at Hubert and said: 'Hush! Or I'll tell Sir Malcolm!'

He did in fact write to Malcolm Sargent who replied on a postcard: 'I'm delighted to hear of my new and unusual fan. Tell him I hope he enjoys Tchaikovsky's Fifth next Monday.'

The cottage is small, and the galley of a kitchen is almost a part of the sitting room; and so when Jeannie was engaged in preparing a meal, she was always being interrupted by her guests. She had a superb way of handling the situation, and however she may have felt, she kept these feelings to herself; and carried on with the banter as if she were not the hostess but the guest.

There was one evening when George Brown, later Lord George Brown, came with his wife Sophie to stay with us for three or four days. George had just resigned from being Foreign Secretary, but he was still Deputy Leader of the Labour Party.

George was a very lovable person, and had the merit of possessing unblemished integrity. He also, unfortunately, had the inclination, sometimes, to be embarrassingly rowdy. 'George,' said Sophie to us one day, 'does have such remorse in the morning.' One night, in his capacity as Foreign Secretary, he attended a ball at Buckingham Palace. He was thoroughly enjoying himself when he saw an elaborately dressed figure near by where he was standing, and he went up to the figure: 'Come on darling,' he said in his rich baritone, 'let's have a dance.' The elaborately dressed figure was the Papal Delegate in his robe.

When George arrived that first evening at Minack, he was in a morose mood, and I thought with disquiet of how to handle the few days to come, let alone the evening. But there was no need for me to worry.

Jeannie, in her galley of a kitchen, managed to prepare dinner, and at the same time carry on a joking conversation with George; he was soothed, and flattered that a pretty girl was flirting with him, and he felt better, and his moroseness disappeared.

Jeannie's gift was the ability to adjust her approach to people, and do so with such naturalness. Thus she was at ease equally with the famous as she was with someone whose life was obviously a struggle. Nor did age matter: children or the old received the same naturalness, and responded to it. Perhaps it was due to her humility, a humility born of her belief that all men and women are not born equal, that some are luckier than others, and she had been lucky.

Hence, at Minack she always gave a welcome to those who came down the winding lane. She realised that they might be nervous, and it was a pleasure for her to put them at their ease. Not even when she was interrupted in a task she was engaged upon did she ever give a hint that she was being inconvenienced. She wanted people to be happy, and kindness was the best way to achieve this. Many, many people have come down the winding lane, and have forever remained a friend of Jeannie.

I have loved watching her subtle ways. I have loved going to a party with her, knowing she would never be a wallflower, always able to match her conversation with anyone present. On the other hand there is the other side of Jeannie. The tough Jeannie.

Occasionally we have trespassers who believe the countryside belongs to them, and not to those who live, and own, and work there, and pay the rates. One afternoon we saw such a couple over on Oliver land, clearly determined to break a way through to the coastal path, and by so doing provide a route for the donkeys, Fred and Merlin at the time, to run away down it, and therefore into mortal danger.

'I'm going after them,' said Jeannie, standing beside me on the bridge. 'And if you stand here with a newspaper, and wave it to the right if the couple are going that way, or to the left, I'll know which way to go if they are out of my sight.'

Off she went, running down the lane, then down the track just short of the Ambrose Rock, where I saw her reach the couple who were dithering.

I could see all three gesticulating as I watched through my field glasses. Then the three turned round, and began to walk back, Jeannie marching ahead. I met them as they reached the Oliver gate opening on to the lane. The couple looked chastened. Jeannie looked glum. They had been rude to her; and she had responded in her Scarlett O'Hara mood.

The contrast between this Jeannie and the sparkling one, lay in such occasions as when she was bantering with someone like A. L. Rowse, the great historian and poet, Cornwall's most distinguished man. Leslie Rowse is the son of a clayworker of the China Clayworks at St Austell, and he is an example of an education in which teachers took satisfaction in lighting the minds of their pupils without being hamstrung by artificial educational standards, or by union rules. Leslie, his mind lit with curiosity by his secondary school teachers, began to teach himself; and from his humble beginnings won a scholarship to Oxford, and then, very young, became a Fellow of All Souls. From then on his reputation soared, and by his own diligence, and genius, be became the most authoritative Elizabethan scholar of our time. Not that some of his contemporaries would agree with this view. Leslie is very outspoken. He annoys colleagues. He hates humbug.

One day Jeannie and I had lunch with him at Trenarren facing St Austell Bay where he lives; and afterwards he took us on a tour of the places in the area which had had an influence on his adolescent life, places like Tregonissey where he showed us the school where he was taught, and the site of the cottage where he was brought up, and where, by a paraffin lamp, he read the great books of literature, studying, questioning himself about the meanings of passages, educating himself, in fact, for the role he would one day play in literary history.

That afternoon Jeannie sat beside him in the front seat of the car. Her questions were alert, stimulating, and he responded with dazzling descriptions of his early life, making us feel that we were living with him again, those days so long ago. But it was Jeannie's manner which stimulated him to divulge his secret self in this way. She acted as a flint. Her femininity, paired with her enthusiasm, made him feel free to talk about his beginnings, excited him to do so. We re-lived with him that afternoon his autobiographical classic *A Cornish Childhood*.

Jeannie always acted as a flint, both for me and those who knew her. Her interests were so wide, and the originality of her opinions sharpened our minds.

'A smile and a word and a drink with Jeannie,' wrote David Cornwell (John le Carré), 'and your writer's block had crumbled at her feet.'

Jeannie and I, over the years, have had a rich friendship with David and Jane Cornwell; and on reflection it seems to have been destined to be so. Two incidents suggest this.

I was with David's publisher one day in London when he said that David was wanting to have a home in Cornwall; and as he said this I had a vivid intuition that, although I did not know him, he was going to play a vital part in our lives.

Then a year or two later, a mutual friend brought

David over to Minack, and we had lunch in the patio on a hot summer's day, the patio which is adjacent to the bridge. David, at one stage, brought up his wish for a Cornish home, whereupon I said: 'Do you hear that tractor? Driving that tractor is a man who has a block of three cottages to sell.' David got up from the table, and set off to walk across two fields towards the sound of the tractor. Half an hour later he returned. He was smiling. 'I've bought those three cottages,' he said.

From that moment there slowly developed a friendship which was to be very special for Jeannie and me. We had in any case much in common. The three of us had all been members of MI5, although David was later transferred to MI6. Jeannie had been enrolled by me as an agent before we married. I had realised her potential value, so had my chief; and so I was able to arrange her exemption from normal call-up on the grounds that she had vital war work to do as Publicity Officer of the Savoy Hotel where the majority of American newspaper correspondents had their headquarters. So we had a common interest with David, and I shared with him the acquaintance of several Secret Service operators in the spy world; and as each spy revelation was revealed, we were able to discuss together the innuendoes. We knew those involved.

Jeannie's *Bertioni's Hotel* was published on the same day as David's *The Little Drummer Girl*; and because he is generous and thoughtful, he brought over in the morning for Jeannie a mixed case of champagne and other wines; and in the evening he and Jane hosted a party which they made certain was a celebration of Jeannie's book as much as for *The Little Drummer Girl*.

David has spent many, many hours in the cottage at Minack, and conversation has flowed, and Jeannie has filled our glasses, and we have all felt relaxed because we knew each other so well that we never 'had laboriously to explain'. We intuitively understood.

There came a day when our friendship was put to the test, and David did not fail us. He too, like all who knew her, cherished Jeannie. And he said this about her:

Jeannie was a woman faultlessly of her time. All her life she belonged to the glitter, the drama and the sacrifice of her time.

She might have died in the war. She knew an awful lot of people who did. Flying bombs nearly killed her three times. But she was tough as well as beautiful, and she took an awful lot of killing.

All her life, it seemed to me, Jeannie wore the unmistakable, almost Churchillian air of a beautiful, well-bred English girl who was ready any time to hop into a siren suit and do some perfectly filthy job. All her life she remained ready to roll up her sleeves for her friends, who included the animals, for whom she had a magic touch, and the countless readers, fans and odd bodies for whom she always had time.

And when she wasn't killed she embraced wholeheartedly the obligations of a survivor.

So did Derek. 'A war had come and gone,' he wrote, 'and I had survived and every day of my life I was grateful. Awareness of the luck of it came to me in sudden moments, reminding me I was one of those who lived on borrowed time.'

Jeannie too remained supremely loyal to her luck. And to her duty towards those who hadn't shared it.

She lived with a determination to make every hour pay. And she did every hour proud, with a courage which was as true to her as she was to life, with straightness, wit and superb style.

And by living so fully, Jeannie kept all her magical variety alive. She got extra years – hundreds of extra years – for being so many people; to Derek and to us.

The champagne girl. The Savoy girl. The girl about town, with a distinctly modern way of selecting her pleasures.

The shrewdie, and the rogue.

She was both private and gregarious. She could bubble away for hours. Or she could share with you the solid companionship of silence, and let the cliff do the talking.

She was frail, feminine, and giddy.

She was industrious, conscientious, and rock-like under pressure. She could be totally unheeding of convention. But she knew the rules.'

We lay there, Jeannie and I, on the mid-March morning which was as soft as a June morning, and watched the white-painted *Scillonian* coming into view, a mile or two off Lamorna Cove, on her way to the Islands. Sometimes we have watched her convulsed in heavy seas, and we have thought of those suffering on board. Today she slid through the water as if she was a yacht in a lagoon.

'What would you do if you were the same age today as when you started on a career?' I asked.

'I don't know.'

'You must have some idea.'

'It's all so different, and yet the same.'

'How do you mean?'

'I mean there were vast numbers of unemployed as there are today, but there were different standards.

There was integrity, and dedication to a job unrelated to the money you were earning. We were not bothered by rights. We may have been mistreated in the strict sense, but this was compensated by the wonderful feeling that you belonged to those you worked for, and there was the intense satisfaction of doing one's best to help. All very old-fashioned.'

'But what would you do now if you were a girl deciding on a career?'

'I think I would try to equip myself to be independent.'

'How?'

'I think I would aim to be a one-person workforce so that I was free.'

'And how would you manage that?'

'Perhaps it would be by way of becoming a super-secretary. I would plan to have three years of intensive training, and I would learn languages. I would spend a year in Germany and France, and then a year on a super-secretary training course. If I was good I would have world-wide jobs open to me.'

'It's a good idea that.'

'But,' she added, 'if I could wave a wand, I would live my life in the same way as I have done, and live in the same age, the most exciting age in history.'

Then she said: 'We always have such fun, don't we?'

'Always have had such fun,' I replied.

The tide was coming in. The waves were lapping the edge of the Bucks, and the gulls were disturbed, and one by one they left, wheeling into the sky wondering where to go, then settling for the calm sea, floating down to it, then riding the water resembling snowballs.

We too would soon have to be away, and cease our wandering thoughts. I looked at my watch, and it was coming up to mid-day. There was still time to talk to

Jeannie about something which had been much in my mind.

'Jeannie,' I said.

'I'm here,' she said jokingly, a few inches away from me.

'I want you to concentrate.'

'I'll try. What about?'

'About next year.'

'Why next year?'

'I want it to be *your* year.'

'That sounds exciting, but what do you mean?'

'All this year, just as in other years you've cosseted me while I've been writing and doing all the other things I have been doing on the land. And when I've finished *The Cherry Tree*, but I don't expect to do this before November, you will be typing the manuscript, and then you'll be doing the illustrations . . .'

'I love helping you. I love doing these things for you.'

'But it's time to reverse the situation, for me to look after you.'

'Why?'

She was coaxing me to argue.

'Only that you have so much talent that you are not using.'

'I don't think I have.'

'Next year will be the chance to prove yourself because next year I'm going to be idle, and I'm going to spend my time looking after *you*. Just as I did when you wrote *Meet Me at the Savoy*. You're going to hide in your studio where you can spend your time drawing and painting, and perhaps begin your next novel which you so long to do and is such a good idea, the story of the luxury hotel suite from the beginning of the century till today.'

'Seems I'm going to have a hard-working year!' she

said, laughing. Then she added: 'It would be wonderful to wake up in the morning, and know that I will have nothing else to do all day except follow my secret feelings.'

'I have another plan, too.'

'And what is that?'

'I thought, after the flower season has ended next year, we would drive to places which have been special in our lives. Your Pinchaford on Dartmoor, for instance. Then the village of Coombe near Oxford, and the house there, where I wrote my first love letters to you, and then to St Albans and Bryher Lodge, and perhaps see Mona . . .'

'How I would love that.'

'It'll be *your* year, and you will decide, and I will placidly agree.'

'Oh I like that! I can see you doing that!'

'But I mean it. And there will be advantages for me because I won't be pushing myself. I'll read the books I have always wanted to read but never done so, and listen to music . . .'

Jeannie laughed.

'A frustrated castaway,' she said,

It was true, I had spent hours and hours listening to records while I was preparing to be a guest on Roy Plomley's Desert Island programme; and have spent much time since, regretting those I did not choose.

Then, she asked mischievously: 'How do you propose to organise the functional aspects of my year?'

'Oh please don't go into details.'

A gull had swooped down on a rock near us, hoping we had left over a piece of our breakfast. There was, as it happened, a piece of bread, and Jeannie threw it to him.

'But I'm interested,' Jeannie said. 'You must have thought this out. How, for instance, are you going to manage the cooking?'

She was teasing me.
'I'll do the cooking all right.'
'Do you really mean all this?'
'Of course.'
She put her hand into mine.
'It's going to be a wonderful year for me.'

NINE

A cool wet spring, and when the cherry tree came into flower there were only a few days of pink glory before a gale came, blowing the blossom away, spreading it like confetti on the flower bed beneath, on the grey chippings in front of the stable, and on Merlin's back. It was a habit of Merlin to stand by the gate close to the cherry tree.

I watched, and felt sad, and curiously apprehensive as I remembered John Masefield's poem:

> Sometimes in wintry springs
> Frost, as a midnight breath
> Comes to the cherry flowers
> And blasts their prime.
> So I with all my powers
> Unused on men or things
> Go down the wind to death
> And know no fruiting time.

Our routine was as it always had been, though muted because of changing circumstances. There was no commercial purpose in growing 3,000 tomato plants as we once did when we had regular help. This year we had only 150, and that was quite enough to keep us busy. Tomatoes were Jeannie's preserve. I helped her plant them, to tie up the strings, fix and organise the watering, but it was Jeannie who cared for them, pinching the shoots out, winding the stems round the strings. I was only involved when the picking of the tomatoes began. Then Jeannie would come to me, saying: 'A basket up there for you to collect. Too heavy for me.'

Sometimes, however, I became impatient by Jeannie's care in looking after the tomatoes.

'Darling,' I would say, 'you're wasting your talents by covering yourself with the green of the tomato plants.'

'I enjoy it.'

'You may enjoy it, but you're still wasting your time. You have so much to give, to do, besides looking after tomato plants.'

She had another fault, if it is a fault, of spending too much time in our galley of a kitchen making cakes and sweets which I told her often I could do without. She was, of course, a great breadmaker, and that was a vital role in view of the tasteless, steamed bread you buy in the shops. She was also a chronic collector of recipes which filled numerous files but were seldom used. Nonetheless she was a very good cook in a non-experimental fashion, and this non-experimental fashion was due to me.

'I would prefer plain roast beef, mashed potatoes and sprouts,' I might say, when she had served some concoction which she had read about in some magazine.

'You're impossible,' she would reply.

When I was writing a book she would take special care of me. I would be irritable, an irritability caused by a mental blockage as to what my next paragraph might say. Jeannie understood, and she soothed my irritability by saying that I would feel better if I had a drink, and she would pour one without waiting for my reply.

She had another drink-giving gesture which became a kind of routine. I have this cabin in the wood, ash trees around me, a magnolia in front of the window, huge holes in the bottom of the stone hedge to the left which look as if they may have been made by badgers rather than by rabbits. I would go there during the winter months after listening to the BBC news, carrying a glass of whisky. Calor gas lit the cabin, and the small heater. A snug place, and I felt comfortably isolated, within an oasis of my own mind. And then, after half an hour or so, a beam of a torch would be swinging round the magnolia and the trunks of the ash trees, and it meant that Jeannie was coming; and she would appear at the door, and I would open it, and there she was carrying another glass of whisky. Whatever the weather.

'How did you *know*,' I would say, as if I had never said it before, 'that I had just finished my glass?'

She fascinated men by her combination of sophistication and innocence. She was capable of behaving as a hostess at a party at the Savoy as if she was born to the role; and she was able to be so easy, so tantalising with a man that he would feel he had made a conquest. Her looks, of course, helped. Her tumbling hair, her fearless eyes, her slim figure which was a reminder of Somerset Maugham's description of a girl: 'she had a body made for the act of love.'

I felt detached as I observed men make the gestures of love for her. I did not feel jealous, and perhaps this is a confession of over-confidence. Other men have believed that their wives would never leave them, wives have believed this of their husbands, but Jeannie and I *knew* we would always be together till the end of time.

Sometimes in my mind, just for fun, I have thought about the men who have courted her. She was always discreet, and clever for that matter, because she never missed a date with me, pretending she had been delayed in the office. A missed date provides the beginning of suspicion. Yet, because we were separated through most of every day when we were in London she had freedom, just as I had freedom.

I believe, if she was with me at this moment, that the man she would want most to remember would be Danny Kaye, whom she knew since his first triumphant appearance at the London Palladium. There would be others, of course, but she was not a person who would talk about them. There was no kiss and tell quality about Jeannie.

Danny Kaye wrote the Foreword to her book *Meet Me at the Savoy*:

> Jean Nicol is a most attractive young woman with all the admirable qualities that made her job (a most difficult assignment at best) an exciting, pleasant and rewarding occupation.
>
> It was through her efforts, combined with the expert personnel of the Savoy, that my numerous trips there were given such a warm feeling of being at home and with friends.
>
> I think Jean has captured the romance and gaiety that is ever present at the Savoy. In this delightful book I feel you will enjoy light reading in its most pleasant form. Here you will find amusing and affectionate anecdotes about people you may not know quite as intimately as you will after you have read these pages.

She saw Danny for the last time when she was his guest at the Royal Command Performance in honour of the Queen Mother's eightieth birthday. She said, when she arrived home, that Danny had been in a pensive mood. His appearance on stage was the climax of the evening and, as always, within a few seconds he had captured his audience. At one moment they were all singing 'Ball in the Jack' and clapping their hands with him, including the Queen Mother, while soon after there was a complete silence as he sang a song on his own.

He did not stay for the after-show party but took Jeannie and some friends back to the Savoy for a champagne supper. As he left the London Palladium, Jeannie beside him in his Daimler, throngs, crowded around it, people shouting: 'Come back Danny! Come back!' But that was the last time he ever visited the scene of his greatest triumph. At the supper party he kept reading out aloud passages from *Meet Me at the Savoy*, nostalgically remembering what he called the happiest period of his life. But he was not just an entertainer. His work for UNICEF all over the world was his greatest achievement, and won him honours from many different countries. But now he was tired, and time was running out. 'He smoked a lot,' said Jeannie. 'He never used to smoke.'

There were no swallows to be seen at Minack, and it was now mid-May. I had seen a solitary one at the end of April flying along the coast above Carn Barges, but there was no sign of any others, certainly no sign of any swallow deciding to make Minack its summer home. Other years they have come, inspected us and remained, but this May I missed their dancing in the sky. The whitethroats had arrived, taking up their positions among the undergrowth of Oliver land, and so had the chiff chaffs. I had heard and seen a cuckoo on 23 April and we both saw a hoopoe, the glamorous bird from Africa. But no swallows. Nesting swallows bring good luck, people say. I found myself praying that they would come.

Every Friday Jeannie went to the hairdressers and, both before and after the appointment, completed the week's shopping. She began early, driving away from Minack at 8 a.m. And when she returned, Ambrose, all-knowing Ambrose, was always waiting for her, and greeting her with those ugly greedy noises which are aimed, supposedly, to entice, but instead earns a 'Have patience!' The cause of his impatience was chopped liver, specially chopped for him by Robert Trewhella, a recent London marathon runner, and son of George Trewhella the Penzance butcher.

After Jeannie had arrived home, she would pass on the gossip she had collected. Hairdressers are dangerous dens of gossip. Men, sitting in the barber's chair looking at their faces in the mirror before them, will talk about football and cricket, and harmless subjects like the stupidity of putting double yellow lines in front of the post office. Nothing risky in that kind of conversation.

Women, on the other hand, view their hairdressers in a more personal way. Hairdressers can be their father or mother confessors. Tongues are loosened as their hair is caressed. Comments are made that are sometimes later regretted. Thus I have said, in my time, as Jeannie set off to a hairdresser: 'Now be careful, don't talk too much!' No need for me, however, to worry about her Penzance hairdresser. Her name was Margaret Laity of Maison Charles in Queen Street. A tall, dark, gentle person. She was a friend. Jeannie was safe and happy with her.

Nevertheless Jeannie would return with gleanings of gossip, gathered during her shopping, true or untrue; and one morning at the beginning of June she returned with the rumour that Jack Cockram, our neighbouring farmer, was thinking of leaving the farm. The news alarmed us both. Jack and his wife, Alice, were the kind of neighbours that people hope for, neighbours of long standing who demand nothing and help whenever they can. I could always rely on Jack if I was in some physical trouble as, for instance, when a visiting car slithered off the lane into the ditch. Not only a visiting car. Both Jeannie and I have driven into the ditch at a certain bend in the lane which lures cars.

On such occasions I would timidly knock on the door of Jack's farmhouse, or call for him in the outhouses, then guiltily ask for his help; and he would get into his tractor, come down the lane with a chain, tie it to the car, then slowly pull the car out. On one occasion when a car was in the ditch the owner came to the cottage to break the news to me, and explained disarmingly: 'I was daffodil dreaming – it was all so beautiful!' Daffodils in springtime line either side of much of the lane.

Jack's partner was Walter Grose whom I have described as a Pied Piper of cats. He does not live at the farm. He lives in the village of St Buryan, and drives to the farm in a little yellow van; and once upon a time a concourse of cats was waiting for him, and he would feed them. The cats are now mostly gone, but a faithful one remains; and now, instead of cats, Walter is dominated by two dogs, Trigger a brown and white spaniel and Whisky, a black and white collie. They worship Walter. They wait for his arrival every morning, and then follow him around on his work. Walter is eighty, but he is young, and has no wish to retire. He defends the basic standards of life, the basic standards of working the land. I have seen him hoeing a three-acre field of potatoes, Trigger and Whisky beside him, slowly, slowly, taking days to do so. No question of him and Jack taking an illusory short cut by spraying the ground with a weed-killer chemical. Every autumn, without my asking, Walter has dug clean the ditch where cars can slither, and cut back the undergrowth. 'Walter,' I would say, 'thank you, thank you, for doing something I couldn't do myself.' And now there was this rumour that he and Jack were giving up.

'Jeannie,' I said, 'this may mean an upheaval.'

'It's only a rumour.'

We were an oasis of a community, happy in our isolation, granite buildings of great age, on close friendly terms, keeping to ourselves but always ready to help each other. No outward signs of modern farming, no stinking silage to pollute the air. Bill Trevorrow living in his bungalow, Mary his daughter and her husband Mike Nicholls, best self-employed builder in the neighbourhood, living in the farmhouse where Bill lived when his wife Cath was alive, then Jack and Alice Cockram. They lived three quarters of a mile from the main road, Minack a further quarter of a mile towards the sea. Life for all of us was hardworking but leisurely. It offered a feeling of peaceful permanence.

'I'll ask Jack when I see him,' I said.

'Do that ... but doesn't it make it all the more wonderful that we were able to buy Oliver land?'

I wonder in retrospect whether some extrasensory power was at work when I reacted so strongly to Jeannie's flimsy gossip. Upheaval? Why should I have used such a strong word? When I saw Jack some while later, he said that he had heard the rumour but it wasn't true. He wasn't giving up the farm yet. So that was reassuring. No upheaval in that direction. Thus, Jeannie and I could continue to live with the comfortable feeling that our way of life was permanent.

Then came a day in mid-June that I had a mild surprise.

Jeannie had picked a couple of baskets of tomatoes, our first proper picking of the summer, and I had carried them down to the apple house, also called the cat's kitchen because it was here the smelly coley was cooked. Jeannie weighed and graded them. They only amounted to three 14lb chip baskets, but the price was high, and I was glad to drive them to the wholesaler in Penzance. It is a proud moment delivering the first tomatoes. One is given a great welcome. One feels important. A couple of weeks later the reception will be different. Tomato production will be in full swing. One is no longer special.

I arrived back, and found a message scrawled on the back of an envelope lying on the table in the porch. It read: 'Gone for a bathe.'

Almost an hour later she returned.

'Oh it was lovely,' she said. 'Why don't you go? The tide is just right.'

I didn't go because I had another idea. Merlin had been mooching around the stable meadow, and I thought he deserved a walk, and I suggested to Jeannie we took him over to Oliver land, and had a walk round the paths, taking the secateurs with us so that we could cut back encroaching brambles. I expected Jeannie to say it was a good idea, but instead she hesitated: 'I don't think I'll come. I'd prefer to stay here and do some gardening.' Then she added: 'I got rather out of breath coming up from my swim.'

So I went on my own with Merlin. I opened the gate to the stable meadow, put on his halter, then led him up the lane, across Monty's Leap, then through the gate into Oliver land. There I took off his halter, and began walking up the side of the field to the gap which opens on to the narrow path which we call blackthorn alley which, in its turn, leads to the Ambrose Rock. After a few yards I looked behind me. Merlin had not moved. A rabbit had caught his attention and, ears pricked, he watched it until it disappeared into a hole in a hedge. Sometimes I have seen Merlin chase a rabbit, even a fox cub on one occasion, and it is for this reason I am always on guard when Ambrose or Cherry is with me, and Merlin is near. There is no harm in his attitude. He is just bored. He wants a diversion.

He found a diversion during his walk with me that afternoon. He followed me slowly into blackthorn alley, having a munch of the grass from time to time on the way, then down we went towards the Ambrose Rock, and came to an area of young growing gorse which reaches up to the wall dividing Oliver land from the next farm where Nellie was the Queen among a herd of Friesian steers. As I reached this spot I could see the black and white steers engaged in their ravenous grass eating – and I also saw Nellie.

So did Merlin.

And that was the end of our walk together.

He dashed off through the young gorse to talk to her, an example of the glorious pleasure of an unexpected meeting during a love affair. I left him communing with her, and walked on to the Ambrose Rock, then along the path all the way round Oliver land. I was at peace except for a nagging doubt at the back of my mind. The path was thick with grass, brambles and bracken were crowding either side of it. The next time I came this way it would be behind the Condor, charging along, clearing the way; and because I am lazy, and prefer to dream rather than to act, I disliked the prospect.

'But you always do it so quickly,' said Jeannie consolingly when I got back to the cottage.

'Maybe . . . but don't forget that the last two times it broke down far from home.' Fortunately I have a friend, Trevor George, manager of John Cooke, garden machinery products, whom I have known for years, and who never fails me whenever a machine breaks down – hedge cutter, Howard Rotavator, Beaver digger, motor chainsaw, electric chainsaw. He arrives within a short time of my telling him. I feel sorry for him, however, if the Condor has broken down in some far distant corner of Oliver land, and he has to push it to his van, waiting in the lane.

Jeannie was having trouble with *Alstroemeria*. Every year we have trouble with the *Alstroemeria*. It is the curse of a small garden. Dormant during nine months of the year, it starts pushing up its green leaves at the beginning of May; and during the following few weeks it drowns every other plant in the neighbourhood. In July it produces, true enough, a galaxy of yellow flowers, but by the end of the month the flowers have died, and the mass of dying pale green foliage is left. Hence they cause an annual dilemma. Pull them up as soon as they appear? The maddening thing about them is that they spread and spread, and although one may pull them up, next year they will appear again, and the problem is repeated as to what to do with them.

Jeannie was performing a compromise. She was pulling up part of them beneath the bedroom window, albeit reluctantly, and she had ready as a replacement a half dozen Busy Lizzies in pots. Instant gardening.

Jeannie has always been in charge of the garden, and she didn't trust me to help unless under her special direction. I have never complained. She it was who pored through the catalogues, ordered the bulbs and the plants, prepared the ground except for the heavy work.

This year she had scored a triumph that had given her special pleasure. She had a weakness for tulips. She adored tulips. Every year she would order collections of tulips bulbs, notwithstanding their failure to appear year after year.

'Curse those mice,' she would say, 'they've eaten them all!'

She had tried various anti-mice ruses like surrounding each bulb with prickly gorse so that the mouse would have his nose pricked if he attacked the bulb. No use at all. She tried soaking each bulb in paraffin. No effect whatsoever. Only too soon after the tulip bulb had been planted there would be a hole dug around it, and only a minced tulip bulb would be seen.

But this year a triumph! Every tulip bulb burst into bloom and the garden was decorated with orange tulips, yellow ones, pink ones; and Jeannie, untouched by rational thoughts, decided that this triumph was due to the combined action of Ambrose and Cherry. They had decided to unite against the menace of tulip-eating mice. They would forget their personal differences. They would catch the mice before the damage was done.

She therefore decided they should have a party, a tulip celebration party. This is an age when we are so dominated by the need to have material-based good sense that feyness does not belong to the modern vocabulary. It is, in fact, a sign of eccentricity. If, for instance, Prince Charles chooses to spend a few days living the simple life, a newspaper calls him Prince Looney. The personal exploration of the mind is considered laughable when viewed from the confines of a city building; and there will also be those who may say that Jeannie was suffering from whimsical nonsense for giving a party to two cats who had saved the tulips. A seafood party; and it lasted all day.

It began with poached lemon sole for breakfast. Ambrose's plate was, as usual, below the bookcase, on a newspaper used as a tablecloth. Cherry's plate was in the porch. Both were surprised by such an unaccustomed delicacy at that hour of the day, and the lemon sole was gobbled. Jeannie, however, had schemed how to maintain the momentum of the party, and there was no question of a quick second helping, despite Ambrose's impatient coarse cries and miaow-less Cherry's imploring look. Jeannie's scheme was to fill their plates little and often. No question of a gorge at one sitting; and in any case the lemon sole was only an appetiser. The Dish of the Day was fresh crab from Newlyn fishmarket, and when fresh crab is placed before Ambrose, he behaves like an alcoholic out of control.

'Calm yourself, Ambrose,' said Jeannie as she placed the first helping before him, 'calm yourself!'

It was odd, as I have said, how Ambrose had come to tolerate Cherry indoors but not out of doors. Out of doors she had to keep well away from him, otherwise he would chase her. Indoors the situation was the other way round. Cherry was the boss, though a timid one. Her reaction, if he came too near, was to spit, then shoot out a paw in the manner of a featherweight boxer making a quick dab at a heavyweight boxer. Psychologically, her behaviour could easily be explained. She was the poor relation. She was a houseguest not an occupant. No wonder she felt insecure. Yet there was no real reason for her to feel in that way. She was enchanting. She was loving. She was full of character.

And both of us were always going out of our way to make a special fuss of her – provided Ambrose was nowhere to be seen.

Jeannie's love for the cats of Minack, and the donkeys, is reflected in her drawings. They are not just outlines of a cat or a donkey. They catch the mood of the occasion. Ambrose is *really* asleep. Fred is *really* grazing. She was terribly hesitant when she was asked to illustrate the first of the Minack Chronicles because she had no training. Hers was a natural talent. But as time went by she became fascinated by the task of choosing what kind of illustration to do. It had to be a point illustration, an illustration which mirrored some aspect of the text, or aspect of our life. Hence there would be the occasions when I would take a photograph to serve as a reminder of a fleeting occasion, such as when Ambrose first jumped on his rock. At the end of *The Cherry Tree* there is her drawing of Fred, for which no photograph had been taken, and it was a drawing that so moved me, so saddened me, that I first said I did not want it included in the book. She insisted that I was wrong.

'It is the best drawing I have ever done,' she added.

I am glad she insisted. It was to be the last drawing she ever drew for the Minack Chronicles.

TEN

'Lane time, I fear,' I said to Jeannie one July morning.

'All right, I'm ready.'

In July the bracken is tall, and bending over into the lane, brambles are spreading their tentacles, and the white cow parsley, and all those other hedgerow flowers whose names I've never been able to learn, are also bending into the lane; and so when a car is driven up and down the lane it becomes decorated with green and white debris.

'I'll go ahead,' I said, 'with the brush cutter, and don't bother to come for half an hour.'

It is hard work and I keep putting it off. Then suddenly I make up my mind to act, and I may choose most unreasonable moments. Such as six o'clock in the morning before breakfast; and then I walk up the lane, the brush cutter swung across my back, the Japanese engine ticking away, driving the cutter bars, enabling me to swathe the bracken and everything else into the lane. It is at this stage that Jeannie's role has always been important.

An hour of swathing, and I am loth to collect the debris; and it has therefore been for Jeannie to pull it into piles with a rake or a fork. Then, when the piles have been made, I will go and collect the tractor, and we both heap each pile into the carrier box at the back of the tractor; and when the box is piled high, Jeannie has a habit of saying meekly, as if asking a boss: 'May I drive the tractor to the dumping ground?' And off she would go slowly, very slowly. She never had total confidence when driving the tractor. She sat on the seat, her back very straight, gripping the steering wheel; and as I watched her drive away, I would have one of those sensations which sometimes well up unexpectedly within one. I would have an unbearable feeling of wishing to protect her. But from what?

I would begin the swathing at the gate side of Monty's Leap, just where I saw Ambrose for the first time, emerging from the undergrowth. Then on I would go up the right side of the lane, past the spot where, on the other side of the hedge Fred was buried; and where, all this summer, a robin was always waiting when we walked past. 'Fred's spirit,' Jeannie would say whimsically. And she would tell people who came to see us, and who would so often be emotionally upset when we told them that Fred had died . . . she would tell them that the robin was Fred in spirit. And then she would give a self-conscious laugh, adding, 'Just a joke of course!'

Then I would go by a small rock which lies in the hedge at the turn of the lane and which a dear friend of ours is hypnotised to hit with her car on her annual September visit. Then up the lane towards the Well, a surface Well on the right-hand side, and which we tap to provide water for the greenhouses by the means of gravity suction. This Well, at Easter this year, had been the scene of a mystical ceremony.

A German couple who called at the cottage knew nothing about the Chronicles, but asked whether I knew of a Well in the area. The couple came from Bavaria, and there is a tradition in Bavaria that couples in love should drink together from a Well as dawn breaks on Easter Day.

I was charmed by such a tradition and immediately

offered the lane Well, and I led them to see it. I did not feel they were very impressed. A piece of galvanised, rusty iron covered it as a protection against intruders, animal or vegetable; and I fancied the couple would have preferred a Well which looked more hygienic. However, they were to perform the ceremony. I went there later on Easter Day morning, and there were the signs of feet stamping on grass around the Well. But there was no message on the piece of paper I had left, inviting them to call later in the day. The Well had served its mystical purpose. The couple wanted to keep that mysticism to themselves.

Once past the Well, I neared the end of our swathing task. The lane became a little wider and the falling bracken scarcer; and I decided to stop opposite the field gate where Jeannie and I once had a frightening experience.

It happened when Fred was very young.

We decided one evening [I wrote in *A Donkey in the Meadow*] to take the donkeys for a walk up the lane, and into a field which led through the top end of our wood. Jeannie, because she has always maintained a wondrous, innocent, totally trusting attitude towards the behaviour of all animals, was not only riding Penny but carrying Lama as well. She had done it a number of times before. She held the rope of the halter as a single rein while a comfortable Lama sat snugly with her two front paws around Penny's mane. Lama enjoyed it, Penny displayed no objection while I, though appreciating the pleasant sight of cat, donkey and my pretty wife, also viewed the whole affair with a tolerant suspicion. It seemed to be asking for trouble. My weakness, however, was that I did not feel strongly enough to complain.

We were in the field and on our way back, a pastoral scene. Jeannie in pink pants astride Penny, black Lama beatific and merging into Penny's black glossy coat. Fred and I a few yards ahead. Nothing untoward seemed about to happen. We were all enjoying ourselves. Jeannie was telling me that Lama was purring, Penny was pausing at intervals to snatch a mouthful of grass, Fred wearing his bright white halter, was taking a great interest in all around. Why this? What's that? In every glance one sensed the gay inquisitiveness of the very young.

Fred and I reached the open gateway of the field, then turned right, down the sloping lane leading to the cottage. It was, on my part, a thought-less mistake. I was so amused by the way Fred was enjoying himself, leading me by his halter instead of me leading him, that I never thought of waiting for Jeannie. The setting was too normal and peaceful for me to imagine that Penny might panic when Fred disappeared out of sight.

Suddenly I heard Jeannie call out. Then I saw Penny come out of the field at the gallop, jump a ditch, and in an instant she was dashing towards me. And to my horror, Jeannie was still astride her, vainly trying to grip with her legs . . . for in her hands she held Lama.

She said afterwards that her only concern was to save Lama. Lama, she visioned, would be trampled upon. Lama was the only one in danger, not herself.

She was slipping to the side on my right . . . my instinct was to try to catch her, cowboy fashion, taking her as she fell, leaving Penny to gallop on. I let Fred go and held out my arms.

But Penny was moving too fast, and she swerved as she reached me; and that was the moment when Jeannie fell.

My hand seemed to clasp her for a brief instant, and then I was buffeted as Penny raced past me. The sound of the hooves disappeared. A rattle of a tractor came from a distance. All was normal again, quiet and peaceful and pastoral, as it had been five minutes before.

I knelt down beside Jeannie, quite still, and her eyes shut, and cupped her head in my hands.

We remembered that incident on this day in July, and how soon she recovered, as we cleared the bracken and the undergrowth from the lane, a task which may have been tedious and exhausting but which gave us both much pleasure when at last it was completed.

We had the rest of the day off. We felt virtuous. The work we had done together justified this. Jeannie sat in the porch drawing Ambrose and Cherry while I, instead of trying to find words to fill a blank page of *The Cherry Tree* manuscript, idly looked through some of our hundreds of photographs. Bundle after bundle of them. Years ago we said we ought to start cataloguing and filing them, and yet had never done so.

It was due to a failing in both of us. We were too haphazard in conducting our lives. We were unable to plan sensibly. We drifted. We have had periods of organising zeal, but neither of us was methodical. Neither of us had any wish to get down to meticulous detail. We relied on impulses rather than reason; and one result of this attitude was these hundreds of non-catalogued photographs, packets of prints without negatives, negatives without prints.

There were, however, the professional photographs which had been simpler to keep in some order. There were many of them: Jeannie at a Savoy function, Jeannie in her office, Jeannie grubbing in the ground at Minack, Jeannie at one of our Boat Race parties at Mortlake, Jeannie helping me pull in a lobster pot, Jeannie with Monty, with Lama, with the donkeys, Jeannie with Gigli who is singing a song to her, and a delicious one of Jeannie at the opening of the Larder in Vicarage Road, Kingston on Thames, the second ever take-away restaurant in the country. Jeannie and I, who had never possessed capital, believed our idea would make enough money to make us independent. It didn't. It was a disaster. But there was this delicious picture of Jeannie at the opening, and I remember how full of hope she was, how full of enthusiasm.

Indeed it is her enthusiasm all through our life together that I treasure. On the Larder occasion I was still attached to MI5, and I was also writing a weekly column for the Continental *Daily Mail*, and Jeannie, of course, was publicity queen of the Savoy Hotel. We had two brilliant chefs who prepared the food: one of them, Bernard Pessione, had been a chef at some time or other in several of the great hotels of Europe, and the other, a lovable, loyal Portuguese whose own great period of fame came when he was personal chef to Alice Delysia who, in her time, was the French Marlene Dietrich. They would stand together side by side, the Larder empty of customers, raging at those who paused at the menu on a board outside, but who did not come in. 'Stupid fool!' Almeida, the Portuguese would growl.

Then, later on in the day, Jeannie, escaping from the Savoy, would arrive, and however bad the day had been, morale was revived on her arrival. The two chefs smiled and were happy. Tomorrow, they felt sure, after Jeannie had been with them for a while, would provide a bonanza; and, at the end of the day, they would pack up, change from their chef's clothes, then set off for Kingston station and home, a happier couple than when they had been alone with me.

Enthusiasm was an integral part of Jeannie's character. How dismal it is when lit by one's enthusiasm for a project or an idea, one is met by incomprehension. It has happened to us both many times, and there has been nothing that we have been able to do about it.

However, I had Jeannie as my sensitive best friend, and when I was depressed, feeling so low that I believed I would never be able to heave myself out of my mood, there was always Jeannie to caress me. There was an occasion when I had begun to write the third of the Minack Chronicles, which is called *A Drake at the Door*. I said to her one desperate day: 'Why am I writing it? What have I got to say?'

And she answered me without hesitation: 'You're writing about enthusiasm.'

She was right of course, but I did not see this until she said so. The book is about three teenagers who became part of our lives: Jane, Shelagh, and Julius, who brought to us one summer all the innocence of enthusiastic youth:

Thus Jeannie and I would be there with these three who had the promise of the years before them, each helping us, each full of secret thoughts and hopes, puzzled, contradictory, timid and brave, obstinate and imaginative. I understood why Jeannie said to me one day that she was grateful for the necessity of cutting lettuces; a humble task, perhaps, but there was more to gain than the prices received.

It was Jeannie's custom to give me a present whenever I completed a book. The present was timed to be given on the day we took the manuscript, tied neatly in a parcel, to the Securicor depot at Truro; and where, in detachment, a clerk would take down the necessary details. It was a strange feeling handing over a section of my life, written about in secret; and from now on out of my control. We would then return to Minack, open a bottle of champagne, and Jeannie would produce her present.

This routine, however, was not to take place in the case of *The Cherry Tree*.

I was having trouble with the turntable of our record player; and one morning I took it to a shop to be repaired, and was told it was not worth repairing.

I was thereupon persuaded to purchase a new turntable of high-tech design and performance; and as I am an impulse buyer, I stipulated I would only have it if a fitter came out immediately to Minack to fix it. Within the hour the fitter had arrived, and the turntable was ready for its first performance.

'What would you like to hear?' I asked Jeannie, and she replied that she would like to hear Leonard Bernstein conducting the New York Philharmonic in Beethoven's Symphony No. 6, the Pastoral. We played it, and the sound was superb. It filled the room as if it were a concert hall, and when the record was ended, we both were silent for a moment. We were remembering that the first record we ever played at Minack was the Pastoral. We played it on an old-fashioned winding-up record player because we had no electricity in those days. But the Pastoral had meant much to us. The music represented the idyllic life we hoped to lead.

'I would like to give you that turntable,' said Jeannie suddenly.

'Don't be silly, it was my decision to buy it.'

'But I want to ... I want it to be my *Cherry Tree* present.'

'I haven't finished the book yet.'

'Doesn't matter, you will – let me give it you, *do* let me give it you.'

I went over to where she was sitting, and kissed her, and thanked her and said the pleasure she was giving me would go on for years and years, filling the room with music, always reminding me of her gift in celebration of *The Cherry Tree*.

The rains came that afternoon, binding us to the cottage, and we were glad because we could indulge in the music of the record player without feeling guilty that we should be doing something mundane.

We played Dvořák's New World Symphony, von Karajan conducting the Berlin Philharmonic; and the haunting melody of the Largo took me back to my father's Memorial service at St Columb Minor Church, near Newquay, where the organist played it. My father was a great Cornishman, and a very loving father. He was Deputy Lieutenant of Cornwall, Chairman of Bodmin Magistrates, and during the War he was for a time Deputy Chief Constable in charge of the Special Constabulary. He was also responsible for creating an underground movement in Cornwall, should the Nazis have invaded Britain.

He had a passionate desire to maintain the essential identity of Cornwall, and he was always on guard against those who were setting out to vandalise Cornwall for their pecuniary profit with modern buildings or conversions in beautiful, lonely places, thus destroying the fabric of Cornwall.

An example of his attitude is forever evident in the lovely Porth Island near Newquay, opposite what was once the family home of Glendorgal, and where my mother was to place a granite seat in his memory. My family had long owned this island but the time came when circumstances forced my father to sell the island to the local council. My father, however, made a proviso that in the event of the sale going through, no ugly cement building such as a public convenience should be erected on the island. The island, he insisted, should remain an untamed island which the public could enjoy. The local council strongly opposed this proviso, but finally agreed. The price, however, which my father received for the island was substantially reduced. My father was an outstanding example to other Cornish landowners as to how they should help, even at financial sacrifice, to preserve the true identity of Cornwall.

What else did we play that afternoon, leading into the evening, while the rain poured down?

I remember Frank Sinatra singing 'When I was Seventeen', and Leslie Hutchinson (Hutch), that marvellous pre-war nightclub singer and pianist, singing 'Goodbye to Love'; and I remember playing a Palm Court version of 'Jeannie with the Light Brown Hair', the song that Carroll Gibbons, sitting at his piano, used to play as soon as he saw beautiful Jeannie coming into the Savoy Restaurant, changing miraculously from whatever music he was playing at the time, the band following him.

Jeannie's taste in music, and mine, had always been catholic in its nature; and the only difference in our attitude concerned the loudness of the music. I liked it loud so that it filled the room, Jeannie liked it quiet. Her ears were more sensitive than mine.

I remember that day listening to the final act of *Turandot*, sung not by Eva Turner, who is the greatest of Turandots, but by Callas whose high notes always worried me. They seemed to warble, as if she was striving too hard. Jeannie's great ambition was to attend a performance of *Turandot* at Covent Garden, dressed for the occasion, and then afterwards supper in the Savoy Grill. But it was never to happen. The opportunity never came our way.

The last music we listened to that day, and it was after supper, just before we went to bed, was a special request from Jeannie.

'I want to remember that wonderful time with Roy Plomley,' she said, 'and how, when the interview was over, we walked back from Broadcasting House in the dying light to Claridge's where he signed his book *Days Seemed Longer* for us. The three of us were as one. Yet we had only known each other for a few hours.'

The music Jeannie had chosen was Rachmaninov's Symphony No. 2 played by the London Symphony Orchestra conducted by André Previn. It was the symphony that I had told Roy Plomley I would like to take with me to my desert island.

Soon after that musical day we went to Falmouth to have lunch aboard the frigate HMS *Cardiff*, veteran of the Falklands campaign. Our host was the captain, Captain Michael Layard, and his wife Elspeth, with whom we had become close friends when he was Commanding Officer of the Royal Naval Air Station at Culdrose. The *Cardiff* was moored alongside one of the piers in the Docks, and her position had a significance for me.

'You see that building over to our right?' I said to Jeannie as we arrived, 'it was there that I parked my car when I was a private in the Duke of Cornwall's Light Infantry, helping to guard the docks. And it was there, when off duty, I used to sit in the front seat writing *Time Was Mine*.'

It was *Time Was Mine* that resulted in my meeting Jeannie. I had rushed up to her at the Savoy, asking her to put the book on the bookstall.

'We've come full circle,' said Jeannie, laughing.

Jeannie was in her usual sparkling form at lunch, and I watched her with pride as she displayed her wide knowledge of life and events; and in particular I was amused by her animated conversation with the great Test cricketer R. E. S. Wyatt, who was one of the four guests. The subject was Bodyline bowling. Bob Wyatt was vice-captain to D. B. Jardine in that notorious MCC tour of Australia; and the controversy had been re-opened recently by a fictional movie of the story. Bob Wyatt was furious at its misrepresentation of events. In Jeannie he found a sympathetic ally.

Next day there was an aftermath to the happy lunch party. Michael Layard invited me to sail in the *Cardiff* as she left Falmouth for Portsmouth the following day

'When we are in the bay,' he said, 'we'll drop you off with the pilot.'

It was an experience of much pleasure until out in the bay it was time for me to leave. Then I discovered that I had to leave by a rope ladder down the side of the *Cardiff*, then make a carefully timed jump into the pilot boat. Just as I nervously clambered over the side, I heard someone say: 'This is going to be interesting . . . on the news this morning it said a man was crushed between a vessel and the pilot boat last night in Liverpool.'

That lunch party was to be the last time Jeannie and I ever went out together. Not that we often went out, indeed very seldom. We did not belong to the conventional social scene. We were happy in our own company, and in the company of those who came to Minack.

The beginning of an end is never recognised except in retrospect. Jeannie's life was as vibrant as ever, delighting people, and being basic by regularly picking the tomatoes in the greenhouse, caring for me, caring for Ambrose and Cherry and Merlin.

Yet, in the middle of August she did complain to me, or more accurately she expressed annoyance, about an occasional pain she had. Jeannie, all her life, had experienced pain from time to time. A dormant ulcer had been diagnosed long ago. She could not, for instance, eat nuts without experiencing an excruciating internal pain. But the tests she had had showed that there was nothing more serious. And her perpetual relish in life seemed to confirm this.

The middle of August was cucumber flush time. There are always too many cucumbers for home consumption or for giving away; and this is the time that Jeannie, over past summers, has turned the cucumber fruit into cucumber soup.

It was a task she did not enjoy; and she used to perform it on the stove in the cat's kitchen (the one time daffodil bunching shed and where coley was cooked). I would carry a bundle of cucumbers to her, and she would groan: 'I can't stand it! It takes me two hours to do soup which is consumed within a few minutes!'

I sympathised with her, but until this particular summer I had been unable to devise a way to help her. The soup, when served by Jeannie at a Christmas party, was a huge success, but Jeannie suffered this distress in its summer preparation.

This summer, however, I had the answer.

'Let's see,' I said, 'whether I can do it in the pressure cooker.'

The pressure cooker was my preserve. Jeannie was scared of it. She would have nothing to do with it. She treated it as if it were a potential bomb. I had tried to persuade her that my prestige cooker with its automatic timing device was virtually foolproof, but to no avail. True, there might be an eruption if you filled it with too much liquid, but then there is always a potential upset in the kitchen if you are unlucky enough to make a mistake.

However, I had proved my worth as a pressure cooker operator, and Jeannie accepted this. Indeed, as a result, I often found myself cooking when, in pre-pressure cooker times, Jeannie would be cooking while I was watching. I had specialities.

My lemon sole fillets, for instance, poached in milk (three minutes) were popular with Jeannie. My beef stew (twenty minutes) was also popular. Then there was the boiled chicken, garnished in the cooker with carrots, rice, parsley, a bay leaf, and a stick of celery that won special praise from her (ten minutes per pound for a boiling fowl) . . . but, in order to serve it as a dish of gourmet standards, I relied on Jeannie to provide a creamy, parsley sauce.

There are other dishes I have produced, enabling Jeannie to sit in a chair watching me, instead of me watching her; and a dish which has given us both much satisfaction has been boiled gammon. I soak a 3lb gammon overnight to get rid of the salt. I fill the pressure cooker half full of water, and into the water goes the gammon along with carrots, celery, bay leaf, parsley, and any other taste-enhancing herb or vegetable. I give it a cooking time of forty minutes, approximately twelve minutes per pound.

Then there is the bonus of a delicious soup. After I have removed the gammon from the pressure cooker, I mush up the cooked vegetables, and pour into the liquid several spoonfuls of lentils. I close down the lid of the pressure cooker, wait for the steam to rise again, and cook for twenty minutes. I am sure I could win a cooking prize with the result.

I therefore was in confident mood when I embarked upon my cucumber soup rescue plan; and my confidence was justified. Jeannie threw her arms around me in her delight when the first effort proved to be a huge success.

My method was as follows: 2 cucumbers, 1 small onion, a large cut potato poached in butter along with the onion for a couple of minutes, a pint of milk, pressure cook for twenty minutes, liquidise, then strain. Return to cooker, pour in ½ pint of cream, season, and bring to the boil.

The whole procedure took three quarters of an hour, instead of Jeannie's two hours.

'I'll never have to do that boring work again,' she said delightedly, 'you *are* clever!'

I doffed my imaginary chef's hat.

'Thank you,' I said modestly.

Her words now haunt me.

ELEVEN

We sat on the rickety seat in the Honeysuckle Meadow, Ambrose between us. We had strolled there before breakfast, the early morning sun warming us, and touching the honeysuckle, strengthening its scent. The meadow has an earth-filled stone hedge on one side, and it is guarded on the other side by a low, drystone wall. Around the rickety seat was a canopy of green leaves from an elder tree; and bushing along the drystone wall, facing the rickety seat, was the mass of honeysuckle.

If I had stood up and looked back, I would have seen the cottage; and if I had been on the bridge above the cottage and looked across the valley, I would have seen the top of the elder tree, bare branches in winter, green in spring and summer. In front of us on that September morning, across the bracken-covered moorland, we looked upon the standing stone and the rugged cliff rocks of Carn Barges; and the sea.

'This is where I want to be when I die,' said Jeannie, 'left wild as it is now, untamed.'

'Me too.'

It was an appropriate place. Carn Barges, where we had stood, seeing the cottage for the first time, standing there in excitement, visioning our future. Carn Barges would be there to watch us when the story was over.

'Aren't we lucky?' said Jeannie, using her favourite phrase.

I realised she was thinking how lucky we were to own the Honeysuckle Meadow. We did not of course own the cottage and the twenty acres around it. But, since we became a tenant of the Lord Falmouth estate on the condition we paid for all improvements, we have done much to change the once-derelict, rat-ridden cottage. We also built the lane through undergrowth to connect the cottage with the main lane; and that was the lane which infuriated my mother and Jeannie when the neighbouring farmer was the first to use it.

However, Oliver land was *our* land, twenty acres of it, and we had decided that any money we had when we died should be devoted to its preservation.

We sat on the rickety seat talking about this.

'It must be preserved,' said Jeannie, 'for the natural inhabitants, the multitude of wild creatures, insects, butterflies, foxes, badgers, nesting birds. It mustn't be preserved for human beings, except for those who seek solitude.'

'You do make me laugh – luring human beings into the countryside is considered very important.'

'The public has vast areas in the countryside to go to, and it is time to think of the wild creatures and their privacy, and the privacy of those who just want to be on their own. Television nature programmes are marvellous to watch, and to learn from. But such programmes make people look not feel – and it is the feeling of the countryside that we can preserve in Oliver land.'

I remembered, as she spoke, that day in the spring when she had been for a walk by herself around Oliver land, and the words she rushed out on her return:

'It was so beautiful there this morning, and I only wanted to feel the beauty. I just wanted to feel the white sprays of the blackthorn, the first bluebells, the celandines, the first buttercups. I just wanted to feel the courting of the birds, the clap of the pigeon wings, the scent of the gorse, the deep pink of the campion. I was part of all this beauty around me. I felt that I was, I didn't think it.'

Ambrose was purring, looking serene.

'We'll have to go back soon,' I said.

'This is such a wonderful moment. Let's not break it.'

We were silent, listening to the purr.

'If we have a Minack Chronicle Trust we would need someone to look after it,' she said.

'Oh, let's not worry about that now. We've got plenty of time.'

'And there's Minack itself to think about . . . supposing a philistine got hold of it, and ruined it?'

'Jeannie darling,' I said, 'stop it. Think of something cheerful.'

'Well,' she said, laughing, 'I'll think of Merlin and his love affair with Nellie. She is such a tease. I'm sure he feels so frustrated.'

There was always a stone wall between them, the stone wall dividing Nellie's farm from Oliver land. We would watch them from the bridge through field glasses, and they would stand there, apparently pleased to be together, and then Nellie would suddenly turn and walk away, leaving a disconsolate Merlin.

'We'll have to find a companion for Merlin,' I said, 'and it will take his mind off Nellie!'

'I think we should wait a bit longer,' said Jeannie. 'Wait until the book is finished and the illustrations. I'd like January to be the time to start looking.'

'Suits me.'

We left the rickety seat, and began to stroll back to the cottage, Ambrose taking his time, but when we reached the big field known as the Clover field, Ambrose played the game he always liked to play when we reached there. Instead of a slow, ambling Ambrose, he would suddenly race past at speed, then come to a full stop, and look back at us, as if he was saying: 'I'm not always an ambling Ambrose.'

We reached the gate opening upon the lane, and as we did so, Jeannie said how much she would like to have a shelter for the donkeys near the gate.

'And for the tractor and other implements,' she added. 'It would mean we had something solid on our land.'

'We will,' I said, 'one day.'

We returned to the cottage, and had breakfast, and everything seemed to be normal and yet it wasn't normal. I had pretended for three weeks that I wasn't worried about Jeannie but I found myself increasingly saying to her: 'How do you feel?' And in a tone that was demanding her to say, 'Fine, I'm feeling fine.'

There was nothing specific to worry about except this recurring internal pain which was like the gnawing pain of a toothache. There were no other illness symptoms. No loss of weight, no loss of appetite, as energetic as ever. Our doctor, a personal friend, gave her appropriate pain-killing pills, watched her, coming often to see her. Jeannie herself was furious with the pain. It was interfering with the rhythm of her life. She never for one moment thought it might be serious.

September is a time when often there is entertaining to do. Jeannie coped with it in her usual warm, welcoming manner. Everything was as usual. Lots of laughter, good conversation, good listening. Nobody guessed that Jeannie was troubled by a gnawing pain. She was not the kind of person to mention her troubles. Other people had enough troubles of their own without burdening them with her own. Indeed, everything that was going to happen to Jeannie was to remain secret. Nobody was to be told, she insisted; and when the crisis came and I had to take her to hospital, then, of course, visit her every day, she still insisted that it should be kept secret. Thus I would pass my friends like Walter Grose and Jack Cockram at the farm at the top of the lane, wave to them; and they never knew I was on my way to see Jeannie in hospital.

She was wearing her red coat, red, her lucky colour, on that day in September when she left for the hospital. It was a morning of thick mist, and while she was packing, I hurried, hidden in the mist, to the Ambrose Rock. I knew there were small pebbles in a crevice, and I collected one, and brought it back to Jeannie.

'For you to take with you,' I said, knowing she believed the Ambrose Rock was a magic rock.

When it was time to leave she first went up to the bridge, and blew kisses towards Carn Barges which she couldn't see because of the mist; and then to the Lama field behind where she was standing, and to the cottage. There was almost a gaiety about her, and she called out: 'I love Minack! I love Minack!' Cherry was nowhere to be seen, but Ambrose appeared, and she picked him up and hugged him.

She went into hospital on a Tuesday, and was operated upon the following day. A major operation, four hours in the operating theatre. But her recovery was spectacular. A day or two later we were told the result of the analysis on whatever had been removed, and it was non-malignant. The surgeon, a kind, dedicated man, said he was delighted with her progress, and that she would soon be leading a normal life.

Within three weeks she was home, as happy and beautiful as ever, and a friend who called, unaware of what had happened, said he had never seen her look so well. We did not tell him of the trauma. We continued not to tell anyone; and when people called during the time she was in hospital, I used to explain her absence by saying that she was staying with her sister. Jeannie was determined to keep her private world secret. Yet it was not a selfish secrecy. She just did not want to inflict her troubles on people. For instance, a week after returning home, she insisted upon keeping a promise to draw the raffle tickets at the fête in aid of St John's Church in Penzance. She performed her duties in a carefree manner. Nobody would have guessed she had been in hospital.

We relished the first fortnight after her return. There were walks with Ambrose to Ambrose Rock, and sunny times sitting on the rickety seat in the Honeysuckle Meadow; and walks with Merlin around Oliver land. It was a very gentle period of our lives, a very loving one. I had a dream one night, a dream which did not run away in the morning, so vivid had it been.

I had a dream of a miniature horseman, clad in armour, riding his horse at speed through a tiny archway. He held a banner in his hand, and he was calling out: 'Jeannie is safe! Don't worry about Jeannie!' I was to hold the memory of this dream in the weeks to come, as firmly as the horseman held his banner.

Jeannie had been told there was no need for her to follow any special diet and that she could eat anything she fancied. Indeed she proceeded to lead a normal though gentle life, so normal that she insisted on a daily typing of *The Cherry Tree* manuscript, a few pages every day. 'It is therapy for me,' she said sweetly when I urged her to let me find someone else to do it, 'and if I didn't want to do it, I would tell you.'

Meanwhile, people continued to call on us from time to time, people who were on our wavelength, kind people, but, without telling them why, I had to watch that they did not stay too long with Jeannie. Unfortunately, one of them, a woman acquaintance who was on a visit to Cornwall, got through the defences.

She arrived in the afternoon, a rainy afternoon, and proceeded to sit on the sofa, obviously determined to have a long gossipy conversation with Jeannie about matters in which Jeannie had no interest. I was irritated but I could do little. She had had an unhappy life, and Jeannie remembered this and, typically, she hid her own feelings and listened to her. It was a fateful occasion.

The lady stayed for two hours, and Jeannie provided tea and cakes, and among the cakes, were doughnuts which Jeannie had bought because she knew I liked doughnuts.

Absentmindedly, as she listened to the lady, she took a doughnut, and ate it. Had she been careful as to what she ate, she might have been on guard – one of those 'ifs' which decorate hindsight. But she ate the doughnut, and the result was great distress.

There is another aspect to the incident. Jeannie, because of the lady's vulnerability, was doing an 'ought'. 'Oughts' often plague our lives. We 'ought' to visit someone, we 'ought' to ask someone to dinner, and so on. And yet all the time, did we but know it, there exist the reversal 'oughts': we 'ought' to ask so-and-so to visit us, we 'ought' to accept so-and-so's invitation to dinner. Indeed when I have an 'ought' simmering around in my life, I have decided I would be wise to ignore it. The pursuit of an 'ought' can cause trouble.

I do not intend to give any detail of Jeannie's problems during the coming weeks, for two reasons. First, they seemed to be surface problems, and when she went back to hospital for a check at the end of October, all tests were passed; she hadn't lost any weight, and her hair had a gloss, and she was full of energy. Second, Jeannie abhorred the intimate disclosures of operations on people, public people or unknown. She could not even tolerate the graphic descriptions of vets operating on animals.

Fortunately, she was being looked after by the doctor, our friend, who was very sensitive. As a country doctor he was accustomed to travel distances around his medical parish; and he would regularly call in to see Jeannie. Often at eight o'clock in the morning. His idea being to make a round of his distant patients before taking his morning surgery at St Just, the tin-mining town near Land's End.

Meanwhile, the work had to be carried on at Minack, and I combined this with the finishing of the last chapter of *The Cherry Tree* by working on the land in the morning, being free in the afternoon, and writing in the evening. A tidy timetable of activity, one might think. Unhappily it did not always work out that way. A machine, for instance, would not start, and instead of progressing with my land work, I would have to tinker with it, even organise a mechanic to investigate. Indeed, this autumn, when for obvious reasons I was anxious for everything to go smoothly, I went out of the cottage one morning, full of vigour, full of determination to get on with the jobs that I had been putting off, and found . . . the water pump had broken down, the water pipe beside the Orlyt had burst, and the battery of the tractor was flat. Indoors there had been other mishaps. Jeannie's glasses had been sat upon by me, the electric alarm clock had fused . . . but the incident which disturbed me most concerned a photograph of Jeannie and me which we kept on the shelf above the bookcase, and which had fallen down on to the carpet. Nobody had touched it. It just fell. A fallen photograph has always sent a chill through me.

The brush cutter, however, worked that day, and I took it down to the meadows where the Obs grow, the miniature King Alfreds, for which Harrods once gave us a special order because they wanted to decorate the Harrods hall with them. I went down to these meadows and motor scythed away, then, after a rest, just sitting down on a rock and gazing out to sea, my mind aimless, I went into the skol meadow where there is a badger set. I scythed away, becoming very tired, my left leg aching because it takes the weight when I am scything; and I was about to give up when, on swinging the brush cutter to my right, I caught sight of a figure watching me.

It was Jeannie.

'Just wanted to see how you were getting on,' she said.

I laughed.

'I should be asking you that!'

'As it happens,' she said, 'I feel so well that I first walked to the Ambrose Rock, then sitting on it, I saw you down here . . . and I just wanted to be with you.'

We went back together to the cottage, and as we were doing so, a foggy mist began to blow in from the sea, and wisps at the beginning thickened so swiftly that when we arrived back at the cottage, Carn Barges was already hidden. How often I have said to a visitor who has called on such a foggy day: 'Over there' – and I am waving towards a hidden Carn Barges and the sea – 'is from where we first saw Minack!'

The mists bring damp to the cottage. All cottages and homes in west Cornwall are damp. For years Jeannie and I took it for granted that a messy moss grew on the ancient, uneven stone walls; and that the books would be damp, and mildew prevail in unexpected places.

Then an enterprising couple who had opened an electrical shop at Wadebridge in north Cornwall, came to us with a home dryer. I was in an expansive mood when they called with the machine, and with Jeannie beside me who was always ready to be in an expansive mood, we bought the machine. This was only a few weeks previously.

The machine was in the process of proving to be one of the most sensational gadgets I have ever acquired. In its first twenty-four hours of operation it collected over a gallon of water from the sitting room, and within a week it had eradicated the messy moss on the walls, and made damp books and damp photographs dry. So when we returned to the cottage, I switched it on. It made a hum, nothing obtrusive.

I outwardly pretended meanwhile to be happy about Jeannie's progress. She was full of energy, typing away at my manuscript, losing no weight, her hair alive – and yet I was worried about her.

There was one evening in November when, after feeding the evening gull as dusk was falling, I walked down to the stables where Merlin was standing with his shaggy head in the doorway. It was a rough evening; the wind was coming from the south, and spattering rain had begun, and soon there would be a torrent.

'You'll be cosy in here,' I said to Merlin when I reached him. Then I put an arm around his neck and began a monologue about my worries. I could never have spoken to a human being as I spoke to Merlin. There we were in the dying light of the day, the rain beginning to fall, the sound of the sea each minute becoming noisier as the wind raised its speed; and here was I feeling safe because I was alone with a donkey. No fear that anything I said would be passed on to another. No fear that I would be misunderstood. I stood there beside him, experiencing a depth of feeling that logic would never be able to accept. I had a spiritual glow as I pursued my monologue. I had a friend to listen to me that I could totally trust. When I was a child I had a similar friend, an Old English Sheepdog called Lance. He too listened to my monologues, and gave me comfort. I was safe with Lance. I was safe with Merlin.

I was not analytically worried about Jeannie because I knew she was being properly looked after. My worry was due to intuition rather than reason. I found myself doing things as if I was being propelled to do them by a mystical force. For instance, I organised the forging of a special gate for the entrance to the Honeysuckle Meadow; and when it was installed, my instinct, a sentimental one of course, led me to say to Jeannie that we should both touch it and make a wish, thus ensuring that the gate would have a form of immortality. I also bought extra honeysuckle plants that autumn, and my instinct again influenced me into making us share the planting together.

In the middle of November she had another X-ray

and check up. She had been suffering from a pain to the left side of her back, and we both were apprehensive when I drove her to the hospital. She went inside, and I sat waiting for her to return, looking at my watch, hoping, waiting, waiting, and then suddenly I saw her running towards me (wearing her red coat), waving, and then I knew that all was well. Nothing serious had been found. The surgeon who had operated on her was delighted that she had put on 8lb in weight, and told her he did not need to see her again until the middle of January. It was a euphoric drive back, and a beautiful moment when, half an hour later, I heard her cry out as we crossed Monty's Leap: 'Home! Home!'

Christmas card time soon began. When Jeannie and I received Christmas cards, we would open them hurriedly, then put them aside, later looking at them again at leisure before pinning them on the beams of the ceiling. We always took our Christmas cards seriously because it required little imagination to appreciate the care, trouble and expense that the sender had incurred.

It was Jeannie for the most part who sent out our own Christmas cards. My job was to try and discover the addresses of the cards sent to us without addresses. This can be a time-consuming effort, and it is prompted by the belief that a card sent must have a card returned. A form of guilt, therefore, drives you on to find the address, and so much of the pleasure of receiving the card is lost. During the previous summer, however, our consciences had been eased when someone who had sent us a Christmas card but had not received one from us said: 'We didn't expect one. We had our pleasure by thinking on Christmas Day that our card was in your far-away cottage.'

While Jeannie dealt with the Christmas cards (our card this year was of a beautiful Ambrose, sprawling on the blue slate ledge beside the flower bed on the bridge), I was coping with the daffodil fields which I strode across, clinging to the handlebars of the Condor rotary cutter. This instrument has to be nurtured because it can hit a rock, and much damage can be done as a result. So too has the driver of the Condor to be nurtured. I am alway thankful when the task has been completed, and I look out on a smooth, plain of a bulb field, now ready for the pickings in the spring. So while Jeannie was dealing with the Christmas cards, I and the Condor dealt with the California field of daffodils, the Lama field which houses the Joseph McLeod daffodils, the Hollywood field, the Dutchmaster field, the Sulphur field, the Early Bride field, and so on. When Christmas Eve arrived I had completed my task.

It was a threatening morning on Christmas Eve, with rain clouds scurrying towards us from the south, and I said to Jeannie after breakfast that we had better go quickly to collect the holly before the rain swept the land.

I took a basket, one of the baskets we used when picking daffodils, and we set off for the holly tree which stands in a distant corner of Oliver land. We have another holly tree, which is more like a sprawling bush, down our cliff. It had always been the source of our main supply before we owned Oliver land, but now we only picked a few pieces from it as a token gesture. The Oliver land tree was of finer quality, leaves of a rich dark green, though neither blossomed with berries.

We walked along the path towards the Ambrose Rock, Merlin accompanying us until we reached the Rock, and there he stopped to munch a patch of grass.

'I'll stay with him,' said Jeannie.

So I went on alone, wondering why she had said

that because we had always collected the holly together.

We returned to the cottage and had a pleasant morning decorating it, and decorating the Christmas tree which stood in the porch. Then we had a happy lunch of smoked salmon and champagne, and we raised our glasses to each other and Jeannie said: 'Aren't we lucky?'

Friends came for drinks in the evening bringing us a record, Schubert's String Quartet in C Major; and after they had gone we played it, then had a quiet supper. We were both sleepy, and I said that I didn't think I had the energy to stay up late to carry out our second formality, that of mincepies for Merlin; and Jeannie agreed. Christmas Eve mincepies without Penny, without Fred, could never have the same magic; and so it seemed reasonable to break the tradition of waiting till near midnight.

Thus we soon put on our coats and went out into the night, Jeannie carrying the mincepies while I carried the torch which I wasn't to need because the sky had cleared, and a full moon lit our way, silvering the rocks, glittering the sea below Carn Barges.

Merlin was waiting for us.

'Here you are,' said Jeannie, dangling a mincepie in front of him, 'and here's another and another!'

We continued to stand with him after he had his fill, Jeannie with an arm around his neck while I had a hand on his back.

'Next Christmas Eve, Merlin,' Jeannie said, 'we promise, you will have a companion. Just wait until after the daffodil season. Then we'll find one for you.'

We were alone on Christmas Day, and all day was fun, sometimes quiet, sometimes a burst of conversation, sometimes listening to music, sometimes remembering other Christmas Days at Minack, with

Monty, with Jeannie's mother, with Lama, Oliver, Fred and Penny. We feel there is a form of spiritual peace at Minack on Christmas Day, as if we are in an open air cathedral with nature as the congregation; and this Christmas Day was like all the others – except that I nearly ruined the Christmas dinner.

Christmas dinner was in the evening, and the turkey had been roasting in the oven for three hours when Jeannie opened the oven door to see how it was progressing.

There was an anguished cry.

'The gas has gone out!'

I had failed to check during the day the content of the calor gas cylinder. I was appalled. I rushed out into the darkness and rain, found a spare cylinder, and heaved it into place.

Jeannie was laughing. She was very tolerant. But I wish it hadn't happened.

I was so anxious for everything to go right on that Christmas evening.

TWELVE

My diary will tell the story.

26 December

All day together. Bliss.

27 December

John Miller came to lunch. We missed Raleigh Trevelyan and Michael Truscott who have shared the holiday lunch with us for several years. They had to be elsewhere. What rock hard friends they are. Michael, whose talents are so numerous, twice the winner of the prize for the top picture framer in the country, a noted potter, a renowned picture restorer, practical, yet a dreamer. Raleigh, author of several books, including *The Fortress*, the story of Anzio, one of the great books of the Hitler war, and more recently also of the Indian epic, *The Golden Oriole*. He was once the editor of my books and editor of Jeannie's first novel *Hotel Regina*; and he is owner of a beautiful house overlooking a creek of the Fowey River. We missed them, and I personally felt emotionally apprehensive that, at this particular moment, the meeting at Minack had been broken. John, of course, was aware of this too because he is such a sensitive person. He is one of the finest painters living, and how proud I was that he and David Messum, asked me to write the introduction to the catalogue of a recent exhibition of his work. To think that the first picture we bought from him cost £13!

Jeannie had a pain in the morning. She said it was like acute neuralgia on the left side of her spine. She made no mention of it to John, and all the time John was with us Jeannie was her usual effervescent self. Yet John, being a special friend sensed something. As he left, dusk was falling, and the evening gull was up there on the roof. John saw it, and I told him the story, how it comes at dusk, always silent, never demanding. John stared up at it for a moment, saying nothing. Then: 'Her spirit will pull her through.'

And he left me wondering.

29 December

Jeannie in her old perky form. A wonderful day. She has started on the illustrations. Took Merlin to the donkey field but he didn't like it. He knew rain was coming, and he was quite right. So I took him back to the stable meadow. Paid bills.

31 December

She had a set-back this morning, and there was a moment of emotion: I heard her say to herself, 'How long does it have to go on?' Then in the afternoon she was back to normal, and she suggested we took the turkey legs, which we had kept for this purpose, to the Brontë Wood for the fox who lived there.

So on this New Year's Eve we went there together, Merlin coming too, nudging us as we walked, a lovely walk which I will always remember, moments like cutting the brambles as we went into the wood, then tossing the turkey legs into the darkened, tree-covered area, where one can feel a part of eternity.

1 January

An extraordinary thing happened today.

We were lying in bed this morning, rain pelting against the window, feeling nostalgic about Fred a year ago, and saying we would have a lazy morning, not bothering to dress for a while. First, however, I had to light the fire, then I found I hadn't enough coal so I realised I would have to dress and brave the elements. I went outside and as I went down the path I looked towards Monty's Leap and saw that the gate across the lane was open. I was sure I had shut it the night before. Then I glanced at the stable meadow gate, and found it wide open . . . and no sign of Merlin. Panic! I had tied each gate by a chain.

I rushed back to Jeannie who immediately said she would get up and join in the search for him. 'Not a chance,' I said, 'mad for you to go out in this weather. You stay here.'

I began searching around the orchard and the wooded area around Boris's hut where Boris the drake and the chickens used to live. Always a favourite place when Penny and Fred used to escape. But no sign of Merlin.

I then walked up the lane thinking that I might find him munching the hedge, but I got to the top of the lane and the farm buildings, still not a sign.

I now began to feel frightened. I have always had nightmares that the donkeys might reach the main road, and get hit. The only thing I could do was to go back to the cottage and take the car out. I gave a report to Jeannie, then I was off towards the main road. It was pouring with rain, a thunderburst of rain, and I had got halfway down the lane from the farm when I saw a little figure in the distance wearing a red woolly hat, and something beside it. For a second I thought it was Jack Cockram, and that he was leading a calf. Then I realised that it was Joan and she was leading Merlin! Joan who first came to help us with the daffodils, then to help Jeannie in the cottage; and who typed the manuscript of Jeannie's *Bertioni's Hotel*, and who wrote the description in *The Cherry Tree* about what happened at Minack while we were away in London.

An emotional scene followed. I was near to tears with relief while Joan was sobbing with tears for a different reason. 'Georgie died last night.' Georgie was her favourite cat. We stood there in the rain hugging each other, hugging Merlin. Then, as we walked back to the cottage, she told me what had happened.

Joan's home lies off the lane which leads to the farm where Nellie roamed in the fields with the cattle; and where in one field she liked to tease Merlin across the hedge. Joan went out of her door, intending to take her dog for a stroll, and saw a donkey walking past her gate in the direction of the farm. She couldn't believe it was Merlin because she knew he had never been outside the environment of Minack; and then she had second thoughts, recognised his shaggy, yak-like appearance, and realised it was indeed Merlin.

What is so extraordinary is that Merlin had never been beyond the farm buildings at the top

171

of the lane. His venture could not therefore be explained by saying he was following a familiar route. What is more strange is that the route he followed was an unusual one. So too his methods.

He, for instance, succeeded in undoing the chain which tied the stable meadow gate. Then he undid the chain tying the gate by Monty's Leap which was easier to do. That tie was almost a token one. I had never imagined Merlin would ever get so far.

Then he went up our personal winding lane, past the farm buildings, then along the main lane for nearly three quarters of a mile, round the corner by Tregurnow Pottery, and to the main road. One would have thought that any normal escaping donkey would then have taken the main road. Merlin didn't. Instead he turned sharp right along a side lane towards Menwinnion Hotel where Jim Williams, author of the classic *Elephant Bill*, used to live.

Halfway down this lane is a chapel, standing at the corner of the farm lane which led to where Nellie had her base. This was the route that Merlin had taken before Joan miraculously found him, close to her home. Why had he done this? What was it that impelled him to go to his Nellie?

I now cheat on today's diary. I only found out a few weeks later the reason why. During that period when Merlin made his lonely, adventurous journey during that night of drenching rain, Nellie was dying.

4 January

Jeannie very depressed this morning, but made happy when our doctor friend called, and made a thorough examination, and soothed her by saying she was going through the trauma of healing after the operation. He is such a dear, so very, very kind. In the afternoon we had a photographic session for the magazine serialisation of *The Cherry Tree*. Jeannie in sparkling form. Nobody could have guessed that she was worried about herself. And she looked lovely. How proud I am of her.

5 January

A young South African couple called, they came from Cape Town, in their middle twenties: 'When I read the Minack Chronicles I feel I am reading a love story,' the husband said.

I suppose it is a love story, but I have never felt self-conscious about anything I have written. I just write about what has been happening. At school I only wanted to read writers who, by their personal experiences, might pass on some knowledge of life to me. I was so shy, so full of belief that my own feelings were unique; and it was for this reason that I became absorbed by the works of authors like Somerset Maugham, and Marcel Proust. They opened up my mind into realising that other people had complicated, contradictory thoughts like my own; and that 'reason', sponsored by academics, had little connection with the realities of life.

This evening we took down the Christmas cards, and as usual when I pulled them off the beam, the drawing pins spattered on the carpet; and I remembered how last year Jeannie worried about the paws of Ambrose and Cherry, not my bare feet.

8 January

We woke up happy and relaxed, and we had slept till ten! Jeannie had a perfect night, then after breakfast she began drawing the first of the two illustrations she was going to do during the day. One was that of Ambrose by himself, the other was a brilliant drawing of the sitting room in our Claridge's suite when we were there last March.

What pleases me today is that she looks so *well*. There is not a sign of illness in her face, and she has lost no weight. Just this nausea after having something to eat.

12 January

Touching, the way Ambrose snuggles up to her at night. He will walk across the bed quacking like a duck, reach her, and burst into a furore of purrs. She cared for him when he was a wild kitten in a way that I would never have had the patience to do. She coped with his growing-up problems, catered for his eccentricities, and fussed over him with her love. How ironic it was that he, distrustful of the human race, running away from anyone who approached him, who took four years before he jumped on a lap – then chose to jump on *my* lap. So unfair to Jeannie!

17 January

She had an appointment with the surgeon today, and she wore her red coat again. I waited for her in the hospital car park . . . but this time when she reappeared she did not wave at me, nor run towards me.

'He didn't seem very pleased with me,' she said.

And we had a quiet journey home.

19 January

She did such a beautiful drawing of the cottage today. Only two more to do. She has such sparkle. She looks ageless. Her illness is an enigma. The X-ray yesterday showed up nothing abnormal. My own belief is that destiny is always in control, and so we just have to wait.

Then suddenly, as I write this I recall that story Jeannie told me, but which I have always kept to myself, never mentioning it again to Jeannie, about the Clacton Pier fortune teller who read her hand when she was a sixteen-year-old schoolgirl, and which she kept secret from her sister and everybody else.

The fortune teller had said: 'You will die in the middle eighties.'

Jeannie, I believe, interpreted this as being in her own middle eighties, not the middle eighties of the twentieth century.

21 January

Illustrations of *The Cherry Tree* completed! They are wonderful, and I said to Jeannie that we must get them off straightaway, and I found out that British Rail have a service called Red Star which guarantees delivery overnight. So we packed the illustrations up, and I took them to Penzance Station. So much effort, so much love went with them.

24 January

She was determined to have her hair done, and I drove her to the hairdressers where Margaret was waiting for her. Then I went and bought a polaroid camera because I had reached a point when I felt I needed my morale to be boosted. I returned to Jeannie and Margaret, and photographed them both. The trouble about a polaroid is that you never have a copy yourself. You always give it away.

25 January

One of the most idyllic days of our lives. We were *so* close. We went to the Honeysuckle Meadow. It was eleven in the morning, the sun was shining, soft air full of sea scents, and a bee came flying around as we sat on the rickety seat, deceived into believing it was a spring morning.

'Oh, I'm so happy here,' Jeannie said.

Ambrose had come with us, and was sitting on the seat beside her, so I took a photograph of them both with my new toy, the polaroid.

'I suppose,' she went on, 'that we both have achieved all that we wanted to achieve when we were in our teens, dreaming about the future.'

'Not many can say that.'

'Neither of us have ever been greedy. I mean we have been thrilled by any success we have achieved, but our ultimate aim has always been to try to have peace of mind. If one is greedy, one never can have peace of mind.'

27 January

Tomorrow she is going into hospital again for a check-up. Joan has been here all day, sympathetic, helpful, such a friend for Jeannie. I went down the cliff to see what daffodils I could pick, and I picked seventy-eight blooms, so she will have something nice to take with her. Just before Joan went home, Jeannie laughingly said: 'I don't expect I'll be away for more than two or three days but during that time *please* paint the bedroom window sills! The smell of paint will be gone by the time I get back!'

In the evening I took a photograph of her sitting up in bed.

28 January

We passed Walter in the lane on our way to the hospital, Trigger and Whisky at his heels. I stopped for a moment, and he peered through the open window and said: 'You lucky man, having such a beautiful wife. Off for the day are you?'

Walter always lavished praise on Jeannie.

He did not know that she had already been twice to hospital. Nobody knew.

At the hospital she found her room was numbered 207. She turned to me gleefully: 'The figure seven – my lucky number!'

When I went to bed I found she had left a note for me on the pillow. It is a note I will keep for ever and for ever:

'My dearest dear, I did not think it possible to love anyone so much as I love you. Thank you and bless you, my darling love. J.'

30 January

I left her yesterday evening in high spirits, but this morning when I got there, expecting to have lots of chatter with her, I found her unconscious. I came back in the evening, and she was the same.

31 January

A quite different Jeannie this morning, really

chirpy. But she insisted that today was Thursday when it is in fact Friday. She had completely lost a day. What had happened?

2 February

St Michael's is a wonderful hospital, organised by nuns belonging to the Roman Catholic Order of the Daughters of the Cross of Liège.

'Everyone is so kind, so kind,' Jeannie keeps saying.

A nurse said to me: 'We are not supposed to have favourites but Jeannie *has* to be a favourite. She is always thinking of *us*.'

Jeannie had the attitude towards the nursing profession that *their* morale should be boosted just as much as the patients'. Nurses have to undergo such terrible emotional pressures, and so Jeannie believed that whenever possible, patients should try to be cheerful.

4 February

I leave Minack each day around half past ten, buy a pasty on the way, and reach St Michael's at Hayle around a quarter past eleven. I stay until about three, do any personal shopping on the way back, deal with any current problems, then go back to Hayle about six, staying until eight or later. Back at Minack again, I feed Ambrose and Cherry, feed myself, and have a word with Merlin.

Today she said to me how strange it was that her medical records had been lost. They had been lost at the time our previous doctor retired. Mine had survived but Jeannie's had vanished.

6 February

It was bitterly cold this evening when I left her, a biting north-easterly. I opened the door of the cottage and there was Ambrose waiting for me. What a support he is being to me; he has an extra-sensory awareness that I need a friend. At 2 a.m. I woke up, hearing the patter of snow against the window, and I had panic. Supposing I was trapped down here, couldn't get the car out? It had happened before. So I disturbed Ambrose, curled up close beside me in bed, dressed, and drove the car up the winding lane to the farm buildings. I would be able to get down to the main road from there if the snow was heavy.

7 February

I had such a happy time with her this evening, and I really felt she was on the mend. I had brought chocolates for the day and night nurses, and there was a lot of laughter. I had also brought with me the invitation we had received to the Hatchards' Authors of the Year Party, and Jeannie began talking about what dress she would wear for it. All such fun, and when I kissed her goodnight, I felt happier about her than I had done for weeks.

Then I left the room, and someone approached me and asked me to go into a side room.

'What do you think of the situation?' I was asked.

'Yes?' I replied puzzled.

'The situation, you know what I mean,' was the reaction. Then: 'Will you be able to cope with what is going to happen?'

I was bewildered. When I had left her a couple of minutes before she seemed so much better.

Now I was being warned that she was dying.

I went out into the darkness and the car, backed it into a stone wall, smashing the rear light. Then I drove home in a daze.

9 February

It is Sunday. The streets were empty as I drove here, and now I am sitting answering letters by the window, and she is sleeping. A dog is barking, pause, it is barking again. Then the hideous electronic bell of an ice cream van rings out. How I envy people who are insensitive to noise. The dog is barking again . . . how can there be a dog owner who can let a dog bark so senselessly on a peaceful Sunday afternoon, *and* near a hospital. The ice cream van has rung its electronic bell again.

10 February

I saw the surgeon on my own. 'You realise it will be a hammer blow for you?'

I was being warned again.

11 February

Ron, Joan's husband, came to the cottage this morning and brought me a carton of milk, bread and a tin of small cakes which Joan had made. I was so grateful.

Then I went off to the hospital, and Jeannie was waiting for me with a bright smile – how dazzling that smile of hers has always been; and she proceeded to tell me how during the night she had woken, found it difficult to sleep, then in her mind began to visit Minack.

'I was lying on my side and knew I was facing

Minack,' she said, 'and every corner became alive for me. You and I know what it has come to mean to people, those who come to see it, finding their way without any directions, and all those who have written to us. I saw it all so clearly. Minack is a symbol, a kind of anchor to those who lead stressful lives. People cling to it in their minds, just as I was clinging to it as I lay awake last night.'

While she had been speaking, an idea had come to me, an idea which had to be put into effect immediately. So I said to her, pretending, that I had run out of toothpaste and I had to go into Hayle to get some.

'*Please* don't be long,' she said.

In fact I raced back to Penzance, to a firm of signwriters, and I explained to them what I wanted to be done, had to be done within three days, cost did not matter. It was of desperate importance.

Then I returned to Hayle and Jeannie, keeping secret as to where I had been.

15 February

I called at the signwriters, and it wasn't ready. Damp weather had prevented the paint from drying. Another two days, I was told.

16 February

'I woke up frightened . . . I don't know why,' she said when I arrived this morning. It was a harrowing morning. She is going further and further away from me, and yet when I suddenly said, 'Give me a smile!' her face lit up with one. I think of that day at Richmond Church when my brother Colin, my best man, said as Jeannie came down the aisle: 'Give her a smile!' She looked the same, the same child-like looks. It is as if she is an exquisite Dresden china figurine which has remained ageless over the years, then is suddenly dropped, and smashed.

17 February

An odd thing happened last night. Ambrose came across the bed, and licked my forehead. He has never done such a thing before.

Then this morning I called at the signwriters, again I found it was not ready. I showed my anguish.

She is slipping away. I rang Barbara this evening, and Jeannie's beloved 'Uncle Martin' (Canon Martin Andrews) and also my brother Colin, and our old friend Mike Oliver who keeps the St Francis Cats and Dogs Rescue Home at Porth, near Newquay. Then I rang Michael Bentley at Claridge's, so that the world where she was thought of as a hotel legend should be aware. On the way home I went to see John Miller and Michael Truscott at Sancreed. So soothing to know they will be giving me real support in the days to come. I am trying to be practical.

18 February

The sign was ready!

I didn't bother about the paper in which they offered to wrap it up. I just took it, and raced off to Jeannie. And when I reached her, to my joy, she seemed so much better than the previous day, and I was able to treasure her reaction to what I had brought her.

It was a two-foot-square wood sign with dark

green background: and in yellow on this sign were the words:

THE DEREK AND JEANNIE TANGYE
MINACK CHRONICLES
NATURE RESERVE

A PLACE FOR SOLITUDE.

'Oh Derek,' she said, 'Oh Derek . . .'

Then she held the sign in her arms, and kissed it. I left it there with her.

20 February

Our wedding day.

I packed into a basket two champagne glasses (the yellow cut-glass one was Jeannie's favourite), and the Asprey champagne opener, along with a half bottle of champagne. I arrived at the hospital around eleven o'clock, and she was in a daze, yet looking so young and beautiful. I started talking to her, telling her it was our wedding day, and suddenly I heard her murmur: 'We're in church.'

Then at 12 p.m., the time of our wedding, I pressed the champagne glass to her lips . . . and she took three big sips. Then she whispered: 'It's lovely!'

The circle is complete. I had yearned we could share one more wedding day together . . . and that she should touch the sign. She will always be a part of it as it guards the entrance to Oliver land.

The sun was shining this morning. Daffodils were spattered either side of the winding lane. Carn Barges was etched against the blue of Mount's Bay. The outline of the Lizard was clearly to be seen.

A gull was on the roof.

A chaffinch expected a crushed biscuit up by the bridge.

Ambrose and Cherry, side by side, no animosity between them, waited for their breakfast.

Merlin was by the stable gate, hoping for carrots.

All seemed as it always had been, always would be. Jeannie . . .

> *The spirits of Minack*
> *Welcome you*
> *To their world of Forever*
> *Where life continues*
> *And death is never.*

A CAT AFFAIR

Derek Tangye

Derek Tangye had vowed never to have another cat after
Lama. Jeannie was different; she was ready to give a
welcome to any stray. When Lama's double appeared on
their doorstep, they were faced with a dilemma. But the
problem solved itself in a mysterious and magical way . . .

SUN ON THE LINTEL

Derek Tangye

Derek Tangye's chronicles of Minack, the Cornish flower
farm where he and his wife Jeannie live, are a major
bestseller of our times.

In SUN ON THE LINTEL, he unfolds another
enchanting tale of their remote and peaceful valley as he
tells the story of his New Year resolutions and how the
creatures who share his life – the ingratiating donkeys,
Penny and Fred; the cats, Oliver and Ambrose;
Broadbent the gull, and a determined young badger –
conspire to help him break them all down.

A QUIET YEAR
Derek Tangye

Derek Tangye's wish for a quiet year is fulfilled in this,
the latest of the Minack Chronicles. In reflective mood he
contrasts his and Jeannie's earlier life in London with the
serenity of the daffodil farm, surrounded by animals and
birds that make Minack so special.

'Let's get back to Minack where our heart is, the
embodiment of a dream.'
Daily Telegraph

THE CHERRY TREE
Derek Tangye

Many people have come to Minack and stood beside the
cherry tree, both famous and unknown. They all have in
common a desire to breathe the fresh, invigorating
Cornish air and share a little in the peace and
contentment of the Tangyes' life.

And their days are filled with enchantment and incident.
In spring the daffodils must be picked. There are Fred
and Merlin the donkeys to look after, especially when
Merlin falls in love. What will be the fate of the first pair
of buzzards ever to nest near the cottage? Then there's
Cherry, the little black cat Jeannie found curled up at the
foot of the cherry tree, starving. Will she be allowed to
stay at Minack?

☐	A Gull on the Roof	Derek Tangye	£4.50
☐	A Cat in the Window	Derek Tangye	£4.50
☐	A Donkey in the Meadow	Derek Tangye	£3.99
☐	Cottage on a Cliff	Derek Tangye	£3.99
☐	The Way to Minack	Derek Tangye	£3.99
☐	A Quiet Year	Derek Tangye	£3.99
☐	The Cherry Tree	Derek Tangye	£4.99
☐	Jeannie	Derek Tangye	£4.99
☐	The Evening Gull	Derek Tangye	£4.99

Warner Books now offers an exciting range of quality titles by both established and new authors which can be ordered from the following address:

Little, Brown and Company (UK),
P.O. Box 11,
Falmouth,
Cornwall TR10 9EN.

Alternatively you may fax your order to the above address. Fax No. 01326 376423.

Payments can be made as follows: cheque, postal order (payable to Little, Brown and Company) or by credit cards, Visa/Access. Do not send cash or currency. UK customers and B.F.P.O. please allow £1.00 for postage and packing for the first book, plus 50p for the second book, plus 30p for each additional book up to a maximum charge of £3.00 (7 books plus).

Overseas customers including Ireland, please allow £2.00 for the first book plus £1.00 for the second book, plus 50p for each additional book.

NAME (Block Letters) ....

....

ADDRESS ....

....

....

☐ I enclose my remittance for ....

☐ I wish to pay by Access/Visa Card

Number ☐☐☐☐☐☐☐☐☐☐☐☐☐☐☐☐

Card Expiry Date ☐☐☐☐